67 PEOPLE I'D LIKE TO SLAP

IAN COLLINS

\Bᵇ\
Biteback Publishing

First published in Great Britain in 2017 by
Biteback Publishing Ltd
Westminster Tower
3 Albert Embankment
London SE1 7SP
Copyright © Ian Collins 2017

ISBN 978-1-78590-135-5

10 9 8 7 6 5 4 3 2 1

A CIP catalogue record for this book is available from the British Library.

Set in Sabon

Printed and bound in Great Britain by
CPI Group (UK) Ltd, Croydon CR0 4YY

MIX
Paper from
responsible sources
FSC® C020471

CONTENTS

For Mum and Dad

PREFACE

Context is everything. For those who have followed my radio programmes over the last bunch of years, there may well be some comfortable familiarity in the following pages.

The mid-'90s felt like a pretty good time to be a Brit. Oasis and Blur dominated the music scene, reality TV had yet to contaminate our minds and we all thought Tony Blair was the Messiah. At the same time, the first national incarnation of the talk radio genre came to the UK. For the first time, Britain was to get its own version of those outspoken radio formats that had dominated the American airwaves for decades. Current affairs and political debate were to be given a makeover, and a handful of famous faces (and, somehow, me) were hired to give the UK a very different choice when it came to the tricky issue of how we digest the big news stories of the day. Phone-in radio had just discovered its own testicles.

At the time, I was fronting the show *Ian Collins and the Creatures of the Night*. The programme was a mixture of topical issues and comedy; a sort of alternative version of current affairs. We were (without realising it) the rebel show, broadcasting through the night to an audience who must surely have wondered if they were witnessing some kind of intergalactic communication experiment. On-the-hoof sketches, a regular cast of call-in characters and a set of vaguely insane features ('I'm Shouting through your Letterbox' and 'Jerk My Chicken Friday' being two of the more questionable) formed the backbone of the show. Myself and my co-twenty-somethings (Mike and Kev) were tasked with keeping the good folk of the UK entertained for four hours a night. 'Wet behind the ears' doesn't even cover it. Regardless, these were golden times and, as far as we were concerned, this was what heaven looked like.

Most significantly, this was the first time that radio hosts in the UK were given the national conch to say whatever the hell they wanted. An open platform to pontificate, moralise and rant about anything they felt was worthy of airtime. If something bugged you, you could simply unload your every thought and observation onto the national airwaves in the form of lengthy (and hopefully compelling) verbal polemics. Harvesting your own collection of reoccurring themes and targets was all part of the deal. The privilege of this position can't really be overstated. *67 People I'd Like to Slap* has now allowed me to transpose my own database of *things that need to be said* into the written word.

The relevance of all of this is that those who have been kind enough to follow me around the dial over these years will know instantly where this book is coming from. The reference points, the humour, the terminology and even some of the specific entries will no doubt resonate.

If you bought this book (and thank you) and know nothing of the above, fear not. There's nothing wildly esoteric about the next few hundred pages; I merely sensed it might be helpful for you to know a little of this backstory. That said, much like the Bible itself, the road trip we're about to undertake can be consumed with or without an intimate knowledge of the author.

Ian Collins
Bromley, 2017

INTRODUCTION

We can all make a list. The things in life that give us the hump. Your fellow earthlings and those unfathomable acts of odd behaviour that are guaranteed to send your head into a super-charged, three-sixty spin. From public figures to the average Joe, work colleagues to services, transport to your own other half. Whichever way you slice it, there's an irredeemable reality here: wherever humans lurk, irrational, dubious and just plain infuriating behaviour won't be far away.

Such acts of annoyance are rarely game changers; they don't usually *matter*. In the grander scale of what is important in our swift lives, these things would never make any serious grade. The tailgater, the noisy eater, the moron with an oversized backpack on the bus, humans who don't know how to queue, or the mere existence of Piers Morgan; none of these things *really* matter to our everyday lives. Yet, at the same time, these relatively innocuous acts are the very things that will raise the blood pressure and instruct our brains to fire up the database neatly labelled *arseholes*.

So who are these people who manage to deviate so effortlessly from the template of what is acceptable human behaviour?

Where do they come from? Are they born? Did they learn this stuff? Is there some kind of environmental component to their irritating ways? Who *are* they?

Maybe we should just blame God. Whatever he was doing on that *first day*, his busy tablet of biblical data clearly didn't extend to removing human idiocy from the gene pool. How did he miss this? This is the man who created fire and water, puppies and fruit. He made little children with cheeky faces; this was a very clever man indeed.

Yet somehow, despite his sizeable to-do list, within those seven heady days he forgot to add a clause which guaranteed that human beings won't behave like utter knobheads. A couple of tweaks to the old DNA and we would have been home and dry.

And so it came to pass that modern life proffers a sizeable chunk of humankind doing stupid things. After twenty years of officially being an adult, I came, with considerable regret, to the gloomy realisation that things were not about to change. The great un-self-aware brigade were here to stay.

I could have festered in such disappointment. The mere idea that I was part of a race where folk were pre-programmed to piss each other off with random acts of odd behaviour was not a revelation I liked. Did I really have to accept that some people simply behave differently to others, no matter how annoying it might be? Should I simply jog on, get over myself and take it all on the chin? Not a chance. Instead, I did what any other confused person might do; I adhered to the words of the great philosopher Justin Bieber. Contrary to some mischievous confusion it was in fact Justin who first used those scholarly words 'don't let things get you down, get up, get up and lose the frown'. God, he's good. And he's right.

In fairness, it wasn't just the sagely Justin who changed my life. My ex-girlfriend Lisa played her part too. Lisa was convinced I was an angry man. I tried to reason that I was, in fact, an annoyed man. Not an angry one. In any case, I had stated, anger is just a twisted form of optimism; angry people just want things to be right. They want people to play nicely. I was pretty darn proud at the last line but Lisa simply took a deep breath and stared at me. It was the kind of stare Michaela Strachan gives to the owners of a euthanised cat on one of those animal programmes.

Lisa's grand plan was that I should make notes. She said that ranting on the radio was all well and good but nothing can beat the written word.

Whatever bugged the hell out of me, I should log it in some kind of diary form. She told me that her therapist had offered similar advice: always keep a journal – put it onto paper. It unclogs the mind and gets all of your angst away from your head and out onto the big wide world of A4. This was intoxicating stuff for me (not least because I had no idea she had a therapist, a man who went by the ever-so-slightly annoying name of Delano). For the very first time I knew what I had to do: share my growing list of exasperation with the planet and expose those knuckleheads whose kooky acts of gross stupidity burden my day. I had to create the definitive list; the unarguable, non-debatable opus.

I know what you're thinking. Different things annoy different people. No two lists could ever be the same. Fair point. One man's annoyance is another's idea of hilarity; my partner can see nothing wrong with Western men wearing bandanas, whereas I subscribe to a slightly different view that unless you have some kind of medical issue or hail from São Paulo, the use of such cranial attire probably makes you a bit of a toss merchant. So I get it, we can all agree to disagree. But *this* list began its life a mile long. It has been prudently whittled down to an irrefutable consensus. This is the *mother* of all lists, the non-negotiable oracle of all things bamboozling when it comes to human behaviour.

●   ●   ●

Along the way I enlisted the help of some friends. Mike, Danny, Laura and Will (The Collective) proved the ultimate sounding board for ensuring I wasn't going totally tonto when it came to the tricky dilemma of what is a reasonable area of abject irritability and what borders on the insane. It's a fine line, kids.

It's important I tell you that the 67 are in no particular order. There's no Billboard-style countdown going on here. I had slaved over the notion that if I created some kind of pecking order I may well be able to stand back and identify some sort of mathematical pattern that explains, once and for all, human imbecility. I had inebriating visions of breaking that code; maybe I would be recognised internationally for my endeavours... '*And the Nobel Prize for finally defining what a dickhead is goes to...*' – it was a nice thought but if the collective brains of Jung and Freud had failed to sufficiently explain away donkey's years' worth of idiotic behaviour then I had to concede that I was unlikely to either.

Literary purists should also take note: there's no smart-arsed narrative going on here. This is on the road stuff: part raw polemic, part diary and quite a lot of general ranting. If I saw it, thought it or it gave me the compelling urge to want to eat my own face, I wrote it down.

So welcome to the journey, my frustrated friends – *our* journey – as we pick the bones, dissect and expose the irksome individuals who taint our daily lives and make this thing called life a tad more stressful than it ever needed to be.

Welcome to *67 People I'd Like to Slap*.

1.

MEN IN GYMS

It all began in the gym.

There are few places that offer richer pickings when it comes to humans doing things that are just plain wrong. From the treadmill to the pool, the sauna to the free weights, right down to the kind of clobber some folk think is acceptable to wear. It's an unalterable fact of contemporary life that when Brits pitch up in gyms, they go a bit strange. Top of the list for high crimes of whack-job behaviour is the den of iniquity that is the men's changing rooms. It ain't pretty.

Unsurprisingly, it's that tricky area of blokes in the buff that throws up the greatest of issues. The human body, in its multifarious shapes and sizes, is *mostly* a thing of beauty: the gobsmacking detail of our delicate brains, the inexplicable moulding of our anatomical form and the billions of neuro and arterial highways are clearly phenomenal feats of nature. Yet, despite such physical and biological awesomeness, that very same anthropological diktat also gave the world testicles. *And* made them look like that.

What the hell happened? Did our creator run out of time? Was it a bet? What kind of cruel world would saddle the entire male race with such pant-based grimness? By any stretch of the imagination, one of nature's most aesthetically displeasing sights. Put it this way, you wouldn't be invited to give any TED talks if you'd just invented bollocks. Which is why it becomes a bit of an international head-scratcher as to why so many of my fellow man-people seem to have zero concern about flaunting their little bits and pieces in a public changing room.

'*Did you see the match?*'

There was only one other person in the changing room. He was clearly talking to me. *Did I see the match?* What match? What is he talking about? And do people *actually* say things like that? – a line I thought had been buried in the misty graveyards of bad sitcoms. Before I had a chance to answer, cliché boy was at it again.

'*We was robbed, man.*'

This was his cue to approach the bench. I knew what was about to happen. A post-match report was coming my way whether I wanted to hear it or not. How could my day have begun like this? A man I had never met was standing two feet away from me banging on about the shortcomings of Mourinho's back four. With no clothes on. It was a disturbing picture. I'm sitting down and he's standing up; the view was not a pleasant one. As he waxed lyrical about Rooney and Mata, I could only sit and nod as his pendulous collection of doom waved from side to side as he became more and more animated. How can this loon *not* know this is all kinds of wrong? How can he be *so* unaware? I'm straining my neck in a feeble attempt to meet his eye-line, but Matey – by this stage hands on hips, like an Athenian model – simply grins with self-approval at the brilliance of his punditry, with not a shred of recognition that his little todger is a mere ruler's length from my head. Where would you have to be on the evolutionary scale to think this was OK?

When you're at home, pants are invariably the first thing you put on when getting dressed. For reasons no one has thus far been able to supply, in the men's changing room pants are relegated to the very last thing. Shirts, socks and even jackets and ties are all dutifully lobbed on before the boxers even get a look-in. Is this some kind of game? Is there a warped alpha male kudos in having your little dongle on display for the maximum length of time?

I had the sense that my new footballing chum may well go on for some time. We hadn't even covered the mid-table matches and I was aware that time was knocking on. Fortunately, help was on hand. My knight in shining armour turned out to be a man called Terry. I say 'shining armour' clearly as a metaphor. There was no armour. In fact, there was no anything clothes-related. Terry, it turns out, was also in the buff and was about to commit willy felony number two. The United fan (whose name I didn't get but strongly suspect was also Terry) continued his musings with his mate Tez.

I was planning my exit when I noticed Terry pull out a large towel from his locker. With a swift *Dynamo*-like sleight of hand movement, he spun the towel into a kind of snake shape and then, gripping the ends with each hand, stuck one leg up on the bench and placed the towel between his legs. He then proceeded to carry out an act that can only be described as flossing your own testicles. Back and forth he went like his life depended on it.

There are so many wrongs here it's hard to know where to

begin. Aside from the upsetting visual component, there are two specifics that spring to mind. The first is that I'm not totally convinced that this is the most effective way to dry one's bits – it all seems a tad hit and miss. The other is that I'm almost sure that none of these oddballs would employ this strange method when they are at home. Nonetheless, and for reasons unknown, it's an option that dozens of men automatically default to the moment they walk into a gym changing room. Again, it's back to that sitcom graveyard – doesn't this kind of nonsense only happen on the telly? Terry continued to floss away for a good ten minutes, all while discussing the plight of Leicester City.

The two Tels are just the tip of a disturbing iceberg. Something damn odd really does happen in male changing rooms: it's like a Tardis where the dial has been turned back to 250BC and previously learnt rules of decency and decorum are spectacularly eradicated from the minds of men. Animal status reigns supreme. Louis Theroux could make a documentary on these places and never run out of material.

When I was a kid, there were signs in swimming pools and gyms listing all the dos and don'ts of the venue – the house rules, I guess: no running, no diving, no dropping litter and the one that made every ten-year-old boy chuckle like a fool, no petting (did anyone *ever* use the word petting?). Each rule was accompanied by a little cartoon of the act not to be broken. I've no idea who dispensed with *The Rules* but they need to return. And fast. And with some crucial amendments specifically tailored to the grim shenanigans of the men's changing room. There are two additions we must add straight away.

The first: *No Bending Over*.

I recently encountered the upsetting spectacle of a man (who looked suspiciously like Eric Pickles) who had decided that the best way to dry his feet wasn't to simply sit down on one of the eighty-five supplied benches but to stand smack-bang in the middle of the changing-room floor and just bend over. This old duffer was as big as a house; it was never going to look good. The upshot of his warped choreography was that the entire room was treated not only to the sight of his ageing arse, but also to the brutal display of his mammoth testicles sweeping the floor like sandbags. It was like the rear end of an African bull elephant – a sight I can now never un-see. This should be basic common sense in a male changing room; never *ever* bend over when you're stark bollock naked. Especially if you look like Eric Pickles.

The other rule: *Please Do Not Stick Hairdryers Up Your Anus.*

It's a hairdryer. It's for your hair. Yet this handy piece of kit, kindly supplied in most changing rooms, appears to have been hijacked by gym weirdos as a full-on body dryer. From armpits to feet, winkles to bums, there's no area of the human body isn't worth an investigative visit from the gym hairdryer.

To compound this grisly picture, folk seem to have not a drop of shame about standing full-on in front of a mirror blowing their assorted cracks and creases in front of several dozen fellow gym merchants. At what point would you not feel at least a scintilla of self-consciousness? Stop it. The last thing I want to see while getting ready for swift workout is Matey in the corner going botty-bound with a Remington.

2.

JEREMY CLARKSON

Putting real people into the list was never the intention. This isn't a diary of *famous* people who deserve a slap. When I'd met with The Collective, the clear consensus was to avoid this area, it was all a bit route one. This wasn't the answer I was looking for. We can all boast our own hit list of annoyance when it comes to those who contaminate our TVs and online feeds, so how can some of them *not* be on the list? My mate Danny (himself an author of some note) had counselled against me including specific individuals. Dan is a kind man and loathes the notion of getting personal. In any case, he had advised, it will only serve to divide the room. I had countered his usually wise words with the point that some things simply cannot be ignored. The pervasive world of contemporary media was just too big and many of those who lurk within it need to be called to account for their unique ability to irritate the bones out of the calmest of souls. Especially this man.

Jeremy Clarkson is a sort of God. The tell-it-like-it-is motormouth of all things car-related. He's the mop-haired jester with a large brain, a fast mouth and the ability to put his finger right on the pulse of a grateful nation. Moreover, he's one of the lads, just like you and me. How can you not adore this lanky buffoon?

There's only one place to begin.

Top Gear lost the plot when it realised the might of its own status. In the world of television, this would normally be the kiss of death. As viewers, we'd loved the cheeky *man-up-ness* of the show (and, let's face it, Clarkson couldn't be more of a man if he grew another penis). We'd chuckled along at those random acts of automotive japery and marvelled at the almost forensic knowledge that these guys had on all matters motoring. But what we loved more than anything was that our cheeky hosts seemed blissfully unaware of any of this; oblivious to their own cult standing in the minds of the many.

But then, as Jezza himself might say: things got big. *Top Gear* went global and our dynamic trio became huge celebrities in their own right. The spell had been broken. The petrol-heads of Sunday night TV had become as much a commodity as the cars themselves. Consequently, the show lost its punch, our hosts lost their verve and each episode now looked spookily similar to the last...

Look, it's Jeremy, the daft old bugger; today he's attempting to race an RAF De Havilland Hornet Moth on a 1970s Raleigh Chopper – let's see how he's getting on...

And here comes Richard, grinning like a weirdo. On tonight's show, Hamster [how annoying is that, by the way?] is going to mount a hydrogen-propelled man-made directional rocket and be fired off into orbit. And let's not forget James, who this evening will look all confused and say things like 'Oh dear' quite a bit while running his hands through his crazy hair and pretending

not to know what the hell is going on despite being one of the
co-writers of the entire gig...

...what is this, *Groundhog Day*? We saw it all last week. And
the week before. And still millions tuned in; the Emperor's new
clothes with added balls.

But none of this matters in the world of Clarkson. Despite
these shortcomings, the six-foot-five bête noire of the goggle-
box has carved out more than just a TV career. Jezza is sought
the world over to endorse, write about, speak to or just shake
hands with myriad outlets and companies. Clarkson, it turns
out, is a workaholic. Don't be fooled by that carefully construct-
ed just-got-out-of-bed, boy-who-never-grew-up demeanour.
Underneath that veneer of public school nonchalance lies a
man with such a burning furnace of ambition in the pit of
his belly it's surprising his arse isn't constantly on fire. When
it comes to media bods working their butts off, JC tops the
list; throw Jezza a bone wrapped in fivers and, like Pavlov's
dog, he'll set to work. In any other world this might be cause
for admiration, but we're talking Clarkey here and that
just feels like all kinds of wrong. There's something chroni-
cally uncomfortable when the nuts and bolts of the man's
psychology are at such monumental odds with his adored
public image.

Clarkson hits the zeitgeist for another reason: his almost
effortless ability to upset folk. The man can't help himself.
Making people cringe or cry is in his DNA. His catalogue of
infelicity and blunder makes for some eye-watering reading.
Black people, blind people, Muslims, women, lesbians and
even Argentinians (we can let the last one slide) have all been

on the wrong end of a Clarkson rant. Each time, the pattern is repeated: Jezza issues an apology, the nation debates the rights and wrongs and *Top Gear* die-hards leap to the defence of their master, claiming that political correctness has gone very mad indeed and the nation needs to get a sense of humour. We then hang around waiting for the next howler.

We can argue for the rest of time about what constitutes offence or what falls into the open space of free speech. But this was the BBC, where getting too close to the water cooler is seen as inappropriate behaviour. It's the Beeb who set the bar and the rules are quite clear: one size fits all. Calling Gordon Brown a *one-eyed Scottish idiot* may well, when deconstruct-ed, be a statement of fact, but try being a junior TV researcher and saying that and see how far you get; you'll be out the door faster than a whippet on crack.

Whatever the subjective nature of Jezza's acidic tongue, at some point he was always going to hit an indefensible bullseye. In 2014, while filming a segment for *Top Gear*, he launched into a rendition of the nursery rhyme 'Eeny, meeny, miny, moe'. With the original lyrics. In the arena of offence, this is Premier League stuff. The use of the 'N' word is about as bad as it gets and a sure-fire path to ruin and oblivion. Even Jeremy himself saw the severity and hastily knocked up a little video to impart his regret. In an apology that even Partridge couldn't rival, he told the nation how sorry he was: 'I did everything in my power not to use that word.' Come on, Jez, don't be a dick, *everything in your power*? Yeah, aside from not open-ing your mouth and actually saying the word. Even by Jezza's standards, this is piss-poor stuff. The BBC were apoplectic and took evasive action. They told him off and gave him another contract. What the hell does this man have to do to lose his job – physically beat up his producer?

In 2015, Clarkson physically beat up his producer. Smacked him one right in the chops after throwing a hissy fit over not being able to get steak and chips for his dinner. For good measure, he also threw in a bit of racial abuse. The line had finally been crossed. Clarkson was fired, the producer (after a visit to A&E) trousered a few quid and *Top Gear* – as we know it – came to a crashing end.

Jeremy Clarkson remained unemployed for the rest of time. The media world took a collective decision that the man was a liability. They adopted a moral stance: you can't continue reaping the benefits and privileges of celebrity while at the same time behaving like a twat. Jeremy went to live in a flat in Bridlington and took up knitting. He was never seen again.

But, of course, that didn't happen.

Instead, the good and great from the dizzy world of international media decreed that the best way to deal with racial abuse, homophobia and knocking people's teeth out is to start a global bidding war and rehire him. In the event, 160 million quid did the trick and Jez & Co. are back with a new show, which is essentially the same old show with a new title. A kind of *Groundhog Day Groundhog Day*.

Additionally, he's also returned to mainstream telly. With a swift closing of the establishment ranks and a healthy dose of absolution, he's once again breaking bread on the talk and quiz show circuit with the likes of the usually sane Jonathan Ross and equality campaigner Sandi Toksvig. The Nigel Farage of light entertainment is back. To coin one of Jezza's own phrases, you couldn't make this shit up. God bless the ratings game.

I had asked The Collective what they disliked about JC. Laura said he annoyed her because he seems to have wooden teeth, something I hadn't previously noticed before but does appear to be the case (what does he clean those things with, Ronseal?), while Mike added that he couldn't trust a man whose best friend is David Cameron – an admirable point. For me, it's all a bit more obvious. Being a fellow media monkey, I'm more than aware that this profession is made up of the mad and the grotesque. A kind of prerequisite, in some ways. But that doesn't mean we should let shysters like Clarkson pass by without scrutiny. There are few other lines of work where behaving like a monumental arse would bring you such heady levels of adoration and such a large stack of cash to go with it. That should sit uncomfortably with anyone.

Check out some of the very early *Top Gear* stuff online and the Clarkson game is beautifully exposed. Jeremy is more Little Lord Fauntleroy than boy next door; his faked-up journey from laid-back posh boy to one of the lads is laid bare. It's more than a tad jarring. And to all those Jezza fans who constantly bang on about him being the celebrity they would most like to have a pint with, think on. Spotting JC down the Rose and Crown at the weekend supping some real ale is not a common sight. The man wouldn't be seen dead with his own fan base. You're more likely to be find him tucked up in the Shires, eating kippers with the Duke of Gloucester.

3.

RECEIPT EVANGELISTS

I've had my eye on this one for a few years now, but it was in the café of the aforementioned gym where things finally came to a head. I'd finished my workout, finally escaped the horrors of the changing room and headed for the coffee bar downstairs to buy a banana. What could go wrong?

As I walked in, I exchanged smiles with the woman who just ten minutes before had been virtually killing herself on the treadmill next to mine. 'I'm gonna burn off six-five-seven' (she actually said the words rather than the numbers) 'so I can 'ave a muffin afterwards,' she had informed me with a slightly over-emphasised grin. And, true to her word, there she was, devouring a muffin the size of Canary Wharf. How close she came to being one of the 67.

I queued up, purchased said banana and headed for the door. That's when I heard the voice of doom.

'Excuse me.'

I turned around to see the girl at the till waving something…

'You've forgotten your receipt.'

My receipt? Is she talking to me? I've just bought a banana. With all respect, why the hell would I want a receipt? I took a swift glance over my newly inflated shoulders. No one there. Just me. And my banana. Again, she beckoned me, cheekily shaking the piece of paper in her hand – this girl was serious. What does she think I'm going to do with a banana receipt? And what does she mean I've *forgotten* it? A word that pre-supposes that on any other day I would have enthusiastically taken my receipt but on this particular day – apparently due to my mind being giddily elsewhere – it had inadvertently slipped my mind. Why the hell is she offering me a damn receipt? Did she think I was planning on returning the banana? 'Look, I know I've eaten most of it and the skin is a bit torn but none of that matters because I have the receipt?' Or did she think I was going to claim for it on expenses? No one ever claimed for a banana on expenses. Even MPs don't claim for bananas. How would that work anyway? In the heady world of accountancy, buried in the fiscal columns of a ledger book, there is no column for bananas. Yet here I was in a weird trans-actional vortex where I was being asked to return to the till to retrieve my declaration of a banana purchase.

I had wondered if there was a way of displaying this incre-dulity via one single facial expression, a kind of international grimace used only for receipt-based debacles. I could sense my temporal lobes twitching; my brain reverting to primal status. This was fight or flight territory. Do I walk away or just shout very loudly? The girl continued her bemused stare, looking at me as if I had just wet myself. I remained glued to the spot, holding in the thousand words that had made their way to the very edge of my lips. After a ten-second stand-off, I cut my losses and legged it.

Despite living in an increasingly paperless society and

contactless systems purporting to address this very issue, the desire to impart foot-long receipts (double if you pay by card) shows no sign of abating. Cashiers and retailers across the land continue to sound off the same infuriating mantras: *do you want your receipt, here's your receipt, don't forget your receipt, here's your change and your receipt, I'll just print off your receipt*. Stop it. Unless I'm buying a selection of iPads, stuff your receipt – I don't want one! Men and women across the Western world are now walking around almost lopsided due to the weight of their bulging purses and wallets all crammed with hundreds of Rizla-thin receipts.

In the last week alone I have been offered a receipt for a burger, a Cadbury Caramel, a single HB2 pencil, a nut and bolt and a cheese sandwich. The miserable list goes on. If I want a receipt, trust me, I will ask for one. If not, let's save some more rainforests and leave the millions of miles of globally issued receipts where they belong: growing majestically up the trunk of an Amazonian eucalyptus.

4.

CHARITY HOLIDAY HOODWINKERS

My mate Lol decided he wanted to raise some money for charity. When it comes to the plight of the vulnerable, Lol has always been more than willing to do his bit. So it was no surprise when he made his big announcement. Lol had decided that in the world of fundraising, he was going for the bullseye. He wasn't about to embark on a sponsored walk around the Dales or spend twenty-four hours sitting in a bath of beans. Lol was going around the world. A trip that would take him 7,000 miles away, to right the wrongs of oppression and civil war. Lol was going to become a one-man Amnesty International, donning a sturdy backpack and embarking on a mission that would make Mother Teresa sit up and blush. At least that's how he first sold it to us.

Lol explained that he was going off to South America to help with the plight of the Cacataibo people. This was a tribal group whose lives had been torn apart by a lethal trilogy of corruption, civil war and industrialisation. They had no voice and little hope. But Lol was about to change all that. The Cacataibo people were about to get a visit from a chubby Brit bearing gifts. Lol was going to work his little socks off to prove to the indigenous people of eastern Peru that some of us in the opulent first world do care.

He'd planned his trip meticulously. He was taking eight weeks off work and was looking for ways to finance this impressive endeavour. Friends and family were only too happy to pitch in and help our mate Lol change the world. I could see the MBE coming his way.

'So how does it work, then, Lol? Do you just turn up and start doing stuff?' We all wanted to know how our new-found missionary chum was going to take on this incredible challenge.

'Well, I'll be gone for just over two months so it's not much time in the grander scale but hopefully I can make a bit of a difference.'

'So is it a case of trying to rebuild houses and the like – getting the schools working and fixing supplies?'

'Kind of,' said Lol. 'But a week isn't really that long so you have to work full-on to try and do as much as possible. I'm totally prepared to put in twenty-hour days if it helps.'

A week?

'Why only a week, Lol? You have two months – surely they won't be setting you a deadline when you're going there to help? That would be weird.'

'Well, the actual charity stuff is a week. After that it's mostly trekking.'

'Mostly trekking?'

'Yeah. It's one week doing the ground work – really important stuff. Then we go off into the mountains and trek.'

'Looking for more of the Cacataibo people?'

'No. Just trekking. It's, like, a massive challenge. Apparently the views on the Inca Trail are some of the best in the world.'

'I'm sure they are, Lol. But what has that bit got to do with the Cacataibo people?'

'Well, by then the charity stuff is done – we then move on to the trekking bit.'

'So, it's like an adventure holiday? One week doing the charity work and then you get to go on an adventure of a lifetime – that we pay for?'

'I hadn't thought of it like that.'

And he hadn't.

And neither do any of the other thousands of bods who do this on an annual basis. It's a cracking concept – get other people to pay for your holiday by crowbarring in a charity angle. There's no other way to slice it, this has more to do with folk lording it up in sunny Peru than with saving an indigenous tribe from industrialised subjugation. Arguably, it's better than doing sod all, but hardly within the spirit of charity and benevolence.

To all those thinking of following in Lol's impressive footsteps, how about using the *entire* trip to give that much-needed help to the Cacataibo people and forget the Bear Grylls stuff? It might not involve smoking quite so many suspicious cigarettes and life-bonding with other trekkers (whom you will never see again) but you will sleep better at night.

At the time of writing, Lol still hasn't disappeared to the other side of the planet. I've also put on hold that recommendation for a gong down at the Palace.

5.

ADULTS READING *HARRY POTTER*

What would you think if you spotted an adult reading *The Gruffalo*? Would you laugh? Wince? Call the authorities? Or just take a photo and lob it onto Twitter? (Definitely the last one.) Similarly, if you asked your mate which book they were reading right now and they replied *Thomas the Tank Engine* (*The Full Steam Years*), you might well consider giving them a swerve the next time they suggested a night out. Which is why I'm still royally confused about the ongoing vogue of grown-ups tucking into *Harry Potter*. And often in public. What the hell happened to a sense of shame? I thought we had put this one to bed yonks ago – we used to talk endlessly about these people on the radio. But with a new stage show, a spin-off film and a variant of the original books, the entire charade has begun again. I can hear those haunting words from that little girl in the *Poltergeist* movie: 'They're here…'

I promise you, I've heard all the arguments: JK is a genius, she's opened up literature to youngsters who had previously shunned it, she's thrown out the rule book, created the most brilliant characters and allowed the imagination of the reader to explore a whole world of fantasy through the simple but effective conduit of traditional storytelling. But hang on, Roald Dahl did all of that for decades but we tend not to see shed-loads of our fellow grown-ups bobbing around the place with a copy of *Charlie and the Chocolate Factory* in their hands. That would be considered very strange indeed.

My baptism of fire into the weirdo world of APRs (Adult Potter Readers) came a few years back when I found myself on the last train coming out of Charing Cross in London. It had been a grim night. Myself and Danny had been unceremoni-ously thrown out of a club due to a miscommunication with the owner – the details are simply too upsetting for a man to make public (save to say nothing illegal on our part) but the club's owner – a terrifying man who looked every bit like he had just failed an audition for Spinal Tap – was unequivocal: we were not welcome back. Ever.

I don't know if you've ever been given a bollocking by a man with long blond hair and thigh-high leather boots, but it's not a pleasant experience. This ejection of injustice had left a sour taste in our mouths so we had agreed to cut the night short and head our separate ways home. Which is how I came to be on the last train feeling more than a little grumpy. And just when I thought my waspish disposition couldn't sink any lower, I clocked the man and woman sitting opposite me both reading the latest *Harry Potter* book. Yes, *both* of them, side by side, grinning like morons, reading the latest addition, *Harry Potter and the Cham-ber of Commerce* (or whatever the hell it was called). This was all too much. Two for one, on the same train? How could my night have ended this way? I'd banged on about this boy wizard phenomenon many times on the radio and here I was, trapped in a train carriage with two of these bods. I needed to digest this.

But things were about to go from quite bad to even worse. As I glanced at the man sitting on the other side of the train aisle, he too was reading *Harry Potter*. And so was the woman sitting opposite him. What in the name of Ron Weasley's wand was going on here? Like a meerkat, I took a subtle look over the heads of the two opposite. And there it was, another eight people, *all* reading Harry. This was beginning to get spooky. Dan and I had sunk a few beers that night but these were not hallucinogenic screengrabs of a lagered brain. This was happening. But *what* was happening? This had all the hallmarks of a B-list horror flick; was I about to be devoured by a carriage-load of Potter-reading zombies? Or was this some sort of karmic payback for upsetting Mr Leather Pants in the club earlier?

My confusion was interrupted by the man opposite, who had stopped reading for a moment, took a sharp intake of breath and turned to his wife.

'I don't think Harry's very happy, dear.' He sneered gloriously at his own critique.

'Oh do shut up,' I thought but didn't say. But the interruption had allowed a pretty substantial penny to finally drop. I'd clocked it. There was an explanation. Turns out the latest Potter book had been released at midnight that very evening. This pack of wizard freaks had dutifully made the pilgrimage to Waterstones in order to be the very first to get their mitts on JK's latest tome.

'I think you might be right,' said his wife, nodding in agreement. The man nodded back, confirming that his wife was indeed right to point out how right he was in the first place. I've never thrown anyone out of a train window before but this must be how people feel shortly before they do. Mate, you are about seventy-two years of age and you have made a journey all the way from Ramsgate (for that is where said train was heading) to stand in a queue outside Waterstones for eight hours in order to purchase the latest endeavours of Harry, the schoolboy wizard. Sorry, mister, but that is questionable on every level. If you clocked me reading *The Tiger Who Came to Tea*, wouldn't *you* think that a bit strange?

My compadres on board the 12.30 are not alone. Across the land, thousands of grown-up human people still insist on a literary diet of *Harry Potter*. And they don't appear to care who knows it. Far from hiding the fact that their current chosen book is a children's novel about broomsticks and slugs, these bods actually seem to get off on it, like it's a badge of honour. A mate of mine, and self-confessed Potterette, once told me that the reason he loves a bit of Harry & Co. is because it doesn't '*suppose*' anything about you (WTF?). I had again countered this nonsense by insisting that the same argument could be made about *Chicken Licken*. He simply glared at me like a cult leader who had just been doorstepped by a TV crew. This is what you're up against.

Whatever is going on here, it evidently isn't about to stop. With these latest manifestations of Rowling's work, the APRs clearly sense a new-found legitimacy. I'm now spotting them again, with alarming regularity. Just the other day I saw one in Leicester Square – *Leicester Square*? The front of these people. That said, there's been a turn of events. Kindle has now allowed these crimes to go unnoticed; who knows what kind of nonsense is lurking on those little screens? The upshot is that the Potterettes can now sit with total anonymity devouring a book that was clearly written for the average reading age of twelve.

6.

SOCIAL MEDIA AND THE BEYONCÉ MASSIVE

How the hell do you begin working out what annoys you about social media? That's like asking what annoys you about Boris Johnson. It's a never-ending list. I could have just written a book called *67 People I'd Like to Slap … on Social Media* and no doubt have the Pulitzer boys banging on the door. But given the many dalliances I have had with the unhinged world of Facebook and Twitter, it would be the mother of all #epicfails not to include a snapshot of just some of the more psychotic manifestations of the medium that has totally changed the way humans do business.

When I first decided to put this book together, social media was still in nappies and there was little evidence that within a matter of years, a few apps on a phone screen would be fiddling so effortlessly with our inner psychology. Today, Facebook, Twitter and Reddit are game changers, up there with the invention of the car and the telephone. These sites alone have completely re-engineered the way we opine, prioritise, self-evaluate and think.

Social media has unleashed a billion opinions, all vying for net space. It's given a voice to the weak, a platform to the wicked and a global debating chamber for the rest of us. For the first time in human history, we are *all* allowed an opinion, regardless of how daft or bilious it might be. In the real world, having a row or a healthy discussion comes with a few ground rules. On social media, it's dog eat dog, a verbal *Game of Thrones* with no realistic prospect of a resolution.

I often put together short videos for Facebook. These are primarily designed to promote the kinds of issues that we might be talking about that evening on the radio. A sort of a tease, if you like. I can record one of these things in about sixty seconds while sitting at my kitchen table. Using the same smartphone, I can edit, add some graphics and, if I fancy, even the odd special effect. I then upload the whole thing to about 100k followers across the platforms. The video then gets shared and within ten minutes about 200,000 people have potentially viewed it. If I then ask a few mates – those with substantial Twitter followings – to spread the word, that figure could reach a couple of million within hours. Just let that settle in. Something I hastily knocked together in my own house has potentially been seen by more people than watch *University Challenge*. Of course, there's no way to accurately gauge just how many people watched *all* of the video or how many fully digested its content, but I can be fairly sure that a reasonable percentage are about to engage with the subject matter. The touchpaper has been lit.

Over the next few hours I can sit and watch hundreds, sometimes thousands, of people post and respond to what I had to say. It's not always pretty. There will be abuse (plenty of abuse), there'll be libel, lots of insults and, on occasion, the odd death threat. Jeff from Durham will pitch up with a muddled and angry opinion only to have it shot down in flames by Lisa in Borehamwood. A man calling himself The TwatBuster will then suggest that Lisa should be incarcerated and have her livelihood removed based on nothing more than crimes of disagreement. Meanwhile, Mark in Eastbourne will post a completely different link proving that all of them are evidently wrong. This was a silly move from Mark, because waiting in the wings is FlanFace, who has the whole thing sussed and provides a counter video to prove his point. Alex, a woman of few words, then posts the single sentence 'You are not worthy' (apropos of nothing) and Jeff and Jim – wrongly assuming it was aimed at them – will tell her to f*** off. Lisa then jumps to Alex's defence and a new sub-debate begins about whether swearing on Facebook is ever acceptable. This is a green light for Sumpy to add to the proceedings by bringing the discussion back to where it began. But his time in the ring is short-lived as Weasel and Kieron, Mike and Chris are all ready to pounce with lengthy missives about why they have all the answers. Within minutes there are 200 people having an almighty row. Some will post their opinion and leave it at that; others will be there all day. Literally all day. And all because I posted a video about why KFC is better than Nandos. This is just one post on one page.

This is not a slight on those who genuinely make brilliant contributions on my own pages. For me, Facebook and Twitter really do provide a great insight into public opinion and constantly supply useful material for the radio. But the point stands: every individual on the planet now has the conch and can post or respond to anything they fancy. And in a world of 2 billion users, that was always going to throw up some gobsmacking variables.

Not a week goes by without someone getting arrested for racially abusing a footballer or threatening sexual violence towards an MP. Every cop shop in the land will testify that 999 is now regularly used to report crimes that have taken place on social media. Being called out to a dispute over comments posted on Facebook is now a pretty standard shout for the girls and boys in blue. Social media has, quite literally, changed the way people commit criminal offences.

It was never going to take long for Fleet Street to twitch. In a world where newspapers are on the wane, the online wall has become a rich source of totally free material. From inappropriate comments made by our best-loved Z-listers to high-profile media types who seem perfectly relaxed about settling their scores on a public network, the SoMe gift keeps on giving.

Then there are the real-life stories: members of the public whose posts are equally valuable for the tabloid frats. From the photo of the girl on holiday having a bikini malfunction – which will inevitably lead to some fashion journalist writing an entire column about what to pack when you go away (and peppering the item with 112 shots of the aforementioned girl) – to the man fired from his job after he called in sick with chronic back pain but then uploaded a video of himself hanging from a monkey bar at Alton Towers. Mundanity, it turns out, is worth more than a few quid.

As more and more people 'take to Twitter' (the papers love that phrase – never used in real life), logging both inane and incredible tales of your life for public consumption has now become as normal getting out of bed. The personal obituary for the death of a loved one, the public row with a spouse, the fundraising page for a sick dog or the money-shot video of a pensioner racially abusing a young Muslim girl in Smiths... the newspapers go nuts for the never-ending supply of folk being folk. The stories are then reposted back on to the very social networks from whence they originally came. The comments begin, the rows start and before you know it there's another ripe story in the making.

If you live your life only through the prism of social media and the tabloid press, you would be forgiven for thinking that the entire world plays out their daily lives this way. They don't. Despite the eye-watering number of people signed up to social networks, most of the population aren't even on them. They have never been to the Zuckerberg paradise that is Facebook and wouldn't know what the little blue bird was if it flew out the back of their iPhone. Even among those who *do* partake, most are passive users.

It's a conundrum the worlds of advertising and media are happy to ignore. These guys fall over themselves for a social media presence. No marketing campaign is worth its salt unless it has a hashtag, no TV show goes to air without its own Facebook page and even nightly news programmes insist on the Twitter tag of the reporter being flashed up on screen. It's an international obsession that has the great and the good playing a global game where nobody knows the rules and few can quantify the benefits. Everyone needs to be part of the revolution, even if they don't know why.

This is how the new world operates, and whether you like it or not, social media *is* a seismic game changer. For those who actively devour every waking moment of it, it's altered instincts and desires, priorities and needs. For those who shun the whole thing, they now have to co-exist in a world that assumes they are just as enthused and as fully signed up as their active counterparts.

Taken at face value, Twitter and Facebook are great platforms to debate, chat and inform. There's never a dull moment. But we also know that these seemingly innocuous threads will also throw up a darker side; unfathomable manifestations of human behaviour that we can be pretty sure would never occur in the real world. I mostly love larking around on these platforms but I find myself increasingly consumed by the desire to gnaw off my own elbows at watching humans behaving like complete Neanderthals. It's for this reason that I couldn't possibly ignore social media when it came to compiling the 67. I've peppered a bunch of these SoMe blunders throughout these pages and I challenge any reader to construct a sane argument that I'm not on to something here. Let's kick off with this howler.

About a year ago, I spotted this post on Twitter.

The First Lady – Verified account – @FLOTUS

Happy birthday to the one and only, Queen Bee! Thank you for being a role model for young girls around the world, @Beyonce. –mo

Michelle Obama was wishing a happy birthday to Beyoncé. All very nice. But something about it bugged me. It was the role model thing. It didn't sit well. Is Beyoncé a role model? Surely that was a matter of debate.

I wrote back to the President's wife.

Ian Collins – Verified account – @IanCollinsUK

Role Model? Yeah, I can't wait for the day my 12 yr daughter gives it a bit of this.

I attached a photo of Beyoncé taken from one of her stage shows. A deliberately provocative pose that showed her in anything but a role model light. I hit send and went back to watching *Storage Wars*. An hour later I logged back into Twitter to see if anything was going on. I had 567 new tweets. Man alive! I don't think I've ever received that many tweets in one hit. Why are 567 people tweeting me on a Saturday evening? I was about to find out what happens when you have a pop at Beyoncé.

From the trailer parks of Texas to the lush mountains of Wyoming, every mad Yank wanted some Limey blood. I had committed the ultimate crime of insulting a singer. Not just *any* singer (as many pointed out) but Beyoncé. As good as insulting Jesus (as many pointed out). It wasn't a pretty sight. Every Queen Bee groupie on the planet lined up for a full-on sesh of Brit bashing. My suspicions of disquiet were first aroused when I read the first tweet:

Please shut the f*** up, you god damn ridiculous British C*** (Classy.)

This was swiftly followed by:

Let's find out where he lives and get someone to burn his house down (Not very nice.)

Then:

You're a dead man walking, or should I say dead man tweeting
(Witty.)

And:

She's filthy stinking rich, and you're a total mofo (Shallow.)

This wasn't looking good but my virtual waterboarding hadn't
even begun. Some doofus from Montana (where else?) decided
to cut and paste my profile photo into the thread for some
added abuse.

You look like a penis with glasses (Quite funny.)

You sure talk a lot of shit for someone with no lips (My favourite.)

On and on it went. All night. There were well over a thousand
posts all baying for my existence to be snuffed from the gene
pool. If I'm honest, I found it all a bit funny – there's some-
thing more than a tad unhinged about people using offence
as a weapon to tackle offence. This point was lost on the Bee-
mongers. I had insulted their god and needed to pay the price.

We could talk for ever about what makes people say rude
and nasty things on a public forum, but that isn't the reason
that I mention the Beyoncé story. When I responded to Mi-
chelle Obama's tweet I deliberately removed Beyoncé herself
from the tag (for the uninitiated, this is called subtweeting).
I wanted to make a point that *my* followers (and Michelle)

would see but I had no intention of sending the damn comment to Beyoncé herself (not that I'm sure she would get to see it anyway); that would just be mean. Yet if you follow the trials and tribulations of Twitter you'll notice that this fundamental error is repeated time and time again.

If you're watching a well-known actor on TV – let's call her Minty – and you happen to think she isn't looking her best, or her performance isn't quite up to her usually impressive mark, it's pretty standard fare to want to tweet about that among your mates. Gossiping about popular culture is backbone territory for Twitter, so there's nothing odd about a warts-and-all discussion between you and your followers; not everyone's cuppa, but all rudimentary stuff in the world of social media. What isn't – *and never can be* – acceptable, is this:

> @Minty – *Hey Minty, just saw you on Graham Norton – sorry, but you look like shit.*

WTF? Why would you want to send someone that? At what point did you think that was OK? Other than making the person on the receiving end feel like a sack of manure, what was the gain or the reason? This kind of casual and thoughtless swiping is standard practice in the world of Twitter.

> @Minty – *love your work Minty but your acting is totally rubbish in this one.*

Stop it. This is deeply unpleasant. What's with the desperate need to want to tell someone *directly* how bad they are? In a gazillion years you wouldn't walk up to them in the street and say that; you wouldn't for a nanosecond think of phoning or texting them with those kind of comments – yet for some reason you thought nothing of doing *exactly* the same thing on Twitter.

The famous, the infamous and everyone in between are more than aware that Twitter will throw up some undesirables; the trolls, the bullies and the deliberately provocative. We all understand this and tend to write it off under the umbrella of basic arseholery. But this is something else. These are the *normal* people casually proffering their wisdom and critiques. People who, for whatever reason, seem blissfully unaware that telling someone to their virtual face that they are crap/unfunny/badly dressed/talentless etc. is socially unacceptable.

So, if someone starts a thread about how amazing the new stand-up sensation Micky Smithers is, and you happen to profoundly disagree and want to vent your anger, that's totally fine. But when you do reply, just make sure you remove Micky's name from your tweet. This way me, your mum, your followers, your boss, all your mates and indeed poor old Micky won't walk away with the overwhelming impression that you're a tactless shit-bag with all the decorum of Katie Hopkins.

7.

PRINCE ANDREW

I've wrestled with the point of the monarchy for ever. Can we seriously continue to justify the existence of this single privileged family? In the modern era, is it any longer possible to construct an intelligent argument as to why the Windsors should remain in such unquenchable opulence? Is it now time to reconsider the constitutional direction of our country? The debate never really goes away.

And then things like the Olympics happen. Laura Trott grabs another bunch of medals, takes to the podium and the national anthem fires up. That's me done. I'm converted back to subject status within seconds. Tingles up the spine, the lot. When the Queen celebrated her diamond jubilee and we had that entire bank holiday weekend of celebrations with the monarch on a boat, Britpop at the Palace and the Red Arrows going crazy in the skies, I couldn't have been more fired up if I had been plugged into the mains. The pomp and ceremony works its magic and all is forgiven.

Whatever its anachronistic nature, the royal family does, curiously, serve some sort of unwritten purpose. We can't quite put our fingers on why, but there's an innate sense that the positive kind of outweighs the negative. Given that our alternative could be President Blair, we sort of have to be thankful for this Anglo/Germanic/Greco collection of regal faces who have, in different ways, been part of all of our lives for ever. I am, therefore, a reluctant supporter of the royals.

With one exception.

If anyone can tell me the purpose of Prince Andrew, you win a coconut. I've scoured and searched, asked and investigated. To no avail. While writing this book I spoke to journalists, royal correspondents and even the odd insider but, alas, it appears to be an empirical fact of life – there's absolutely no point in the Duke of York. He serves no purpose whatsoever.

A couple of years ago we were told that the prince was crucial to the UK's relationship with the international business community. He was drafted in by the Business Department to jet around the globe to grin and press the flesh with a variety of bigwigs from the world of commerce and industry. The idea being that if a large corporation was in doubt about whether to give that big contract to the French or to us, we would send over Andrew to gawp at some folk and hopefully clinch the deal. I have yet to see a single example of any contracts or million-pound business transactions that were secured solely via the appearance of Andy at the conference table. In fact, many argue that his presence has been more of a hindrance. Given that two of his best mates on the global circuit were Saif Gaddafi and the international gun smuggler Tarek Kaituni, it's easy to see why. Not exactly a glowing CV when it comes to how to win friends and influence people.

Undeterred, the prince was more than keen to show the world that he should be taken very seriously and that he wasn't merely a sponger of the royal purse who spent the best part of his day on a golf course and rest of it bed-hopping with glamour girls on the party scene. His reinvention was short-lived after it was discovered that the dicey duke had even more interesting friends up his sleeve, including convicted paedophile and human rights abuser Jeffrey Epstein, who was jailed back in 2008 for soliciting an underage girl for the purposes of prostitution, and Ilham Aliyev, the President of Azerbaijan, a man who has so many allegations of human rights abuses against him that Amnesty International can't fit them all on the charge sheet. The prince remains friends with both of these pillars of the global community, and public coffers are regularly used to finance visits to see his chums.

It all sounds like a bad plot from a remake of 24. Remember, this is a man who is paid for by *us*. He's meant to be serving a purpose for the good of the United Kingdom. Isn't being sixth in line to the throne a bit of a serious gig? Die-hard royalists are always quick to point out the level of importance we should attach to the extended royal family and how, behind the scenes, they are working their socks off for the common good. Really?

I should be able to sit here and write an admirable précis about what our diligent duke does on regular basis for a grateful nation. Every Brit should be able to reel off a list of the prince's charitable endeavours as automatically as we can recite the alphabet. Any man who is paid that much dosh by the very people he is supposed to serve should be as visible a presence on our radars as Graham Norton.

Instead, when I think of Prince Andrew I'm reminded of his relationship with a soft-porn star, shady business deals with tyrants and murderers, a penchant for fast cars, a million-dollar global property empire and having several jollies a year with that ginger woman he was once married to.

So I'll keep on waving that flag whenever Her Maj turns up on the balcony at Buck House but, if it's all the same, I'll save the official one-fingered salute for the serial philanderer and chief sponge merchant that is His Royal Highness, the Duke of York.

8.

BRITS USING CHOPSTICKS

Sometimes, honesty really is the best policy. If you go into most Chinese restaurants (other than in Bromley, where the savvy Chinese have already sussed this ridiculous spectacle), you'll be offered a pair of nicely wrapped-up chopsticks. What better way to get into the authentic vibe of oriental cuisine than using the traditional method of two sticks to eat your dinner? The Chinese have been munching away like this since the Xia Dynasty. Or, in more digestible parlance, for 4,000 years. Brits have been giving it a go since about 1978.

The marriage between food and sticks is not a happy one for us Brits. It's in neither our culture nor our instincts. Yet, night after night, thousands of us scoot along to our favourite Chinese Parlour with a view to going nosh crazy with two bits of wood. And 95 per cent of us will look like prize turnips when we try. If you've never had a good look around at your fellow diners in your local Chinese, please give it a go. It's an education. It will also enhance any dull evening by watching your follow Brits virtually dislocate their own fingers while trying to tuck into a bowl of rice using chopsticks.

I once saw some numpty almost tie a reef knot with his own

thumb and index finger while trying to capture some tricky noodles. It was not a happy sight and took the poor man a good thirty attempts to eat the equivalent of one helping. He eventually settled on holding one stick in each hand, thinking it might be some kind of happy compromise. Just use a knife and fork, damn it – no one will think any less of you. Even those who consider themselves masters of the chopstick (and don't they just *love* their diverse abilities) will, if you ask them nicely, concede that contorting their digits and playing diablo with a prawn ball is probably not the most efficient way of eating a meal.

Not being able to use chopsticks is not a matter of shame. You aren't culturally impotent because you haven't mastered this art, no more than you should be questioned because you can't order gong bao chicken in fluent Mandarin. So 'fess up, discard the sticks and enjoy that sizzling number 86 via the conventions of a knife and fork. You know you want to.

9.

DODGY PARENTS AT
SCHOOL SPORTS DAYS

I spotted the culprit early doors. He was standing inside the perimeter of the school playing field in a Nike top, snazzy Adidas trainers and a sweatband on his head. The attire looked new. He was pacing, and then running, alongside the school fence. Back and forth he went, like a pro footballer warming up for the inevitable substitution. Once in a while he would stop to assess his surroundings. It wouldn't be long now. As kids jumped into sacks and parents yelled with delight, the man at the fence remained focused. He was onto stretches now – three to the left, three to the right. He looked to the sky, as if searching for some celestial inspiration. He then took several meaningful deep breaths. Hands on hips now. It was just a matter of time.

With the sack race concluded and medals placed over the tiny shoulders of the racers, the head teacher took to the microphone.

'And now, everybody, we move on to a very important part of the day. It's the dads' race.' (Whoops all round.)

The man at the fence couldn't have sprung into more

purposeful action if they had fired up the *Rocky* theme. His time had come.

As several slightly overweight and beautifully unprepared dads made their way to the starting line, Bromley's answer to Usain Bolt began his mission. As the other dads joshed and bantered, the man with the super-soft Nikes simply retained his composure and said nothing. He scraped his heel on the chalk starting line, marking his territory for the big show-down. As the other fathers took to their lanes, the head teacher prepared for blast-off.

'On your marks…'

It was at this point that Super Dad assumed an almost horizontal crouch, like a massive frog preparing for launch.

'Get set…'

He looked ahead and took in one final breath. The breath of a winner.

The whistle sounded. And they were off. Usain took an early lead. His months of practice were clearly paying dividends and he was already a good three metres ahead of the others. Fatty Arbuckle in lane one had dropped out almost immediately (to some polite applause), while lanes five, six, and seven made it clear from the outset that they didn't give a toss and were playing it for laughs. Good on them. This left just three run-ners. As we moved to the halfway mark, one dad began to flag. This had now become a two-man race: our fella in the shiny clobber and another, whose slightly clumsy demeanour be-trayed his sprightly ability on the track. They were running for their lives. This was going to be close. Only twenty metres to go now, but Super Dad had started to look troubled; his face was contorting badly – the look of a man who had just had a red-hot poker inserted into his bottom. But he wasn't giving up. Those last final sprints were crucial. No pain, no gain. This was excruciating as both men mustered all they could in order to tap their toe over the line. It couldn't have been closer. The race was over.

There seemed to be commotion afoot. The two runners were huddled into a conversation with the head teacher. One of the other dads had joined the mêlée. Something had gone badly wrong. Turns out that the head had called it a tie, a dead heat, she said. And in the name of sportsmanship (added to which this was a school sports day, not Rio 2016), she had decided, in the spirit of fun, to give both men a medal. The crowd showed some lukewarm appreciation for the two dads as they made their way back to their respective families. No handshakes. I noticed Shiny Shorts remove his medal as he approached his devastated family, the shame complete.

We often mull over what ingredients make up our wide and varied human gene pool. Why are some people inherently bad? Why are others constantly happy? Why do some get nervous while others ooze an unbridled confidence? And there's another question psychologists should add to that tricky list: why do some parents at school sports days behave like utter wankers?

Earlier on the same day, a woman had complained about what she saw as an unfair call in the egg and spoon race. Her kid had come second but she was quick to point out that this was only because the eventual winner had been allowed to replace his egg onto the spoon after it had dropped for a *third* time – this should have disqualified the little cheat and, as a consequence, her girl would rightly be the egg and spoon champion. The panel had ruled against her and little Pandora had to settle for second best. Her mum scuttled off, looking like someone had just killed her dog.

As the day ended and we all made our way home, I noticed little Pandora holding her dad's hand. The picture could hardly have been more complete. It turned out that her dad was none other than Usain, our not so super-fast arseclown in the Nike boots.

10.

OWEN JONES

For the uninitiated, Owen Jones is a left-wing journalist who writes stuff for *The Guardian*. Owen is old-school Labour; more left-wing than an Albanian Keep Left sign, and proud of it. In Owen's world, Karl Marx would be the King and Hilda Gadea the Queen (in a clear re-working of the definition of royalty given the anti-monarchistic nature of this ideology) and a large red flag would fly proudly over the Palace. The rich and successful would be taxed out of their own pants and the minimum wage would be two hundred and fifty quid an hour. You get the picture.

Nothing wrong with any of that. We live in a wonderful democracy and the spectrum of political choice should be wide. Recent elections have proffered such parties as the Church of The Militant Elvis Party and the Teddy Bear Alliance – why shouldn't Owen and his friends have theirs? Jonesy is essentially the left-wing equivalent of a UKIP voter: part passion, part revisionist and part bonkers. Again, this is all fine, freedom of speech and all that. As the political dynamic of our country has changed, and Jeremy Corbyn's Labour has reshaped the terms of debate, OJ has found himself very much in demand on the TV and radio news circuit.

There's an angry narrative out there right now. The anti-banker, anti-MP vibe is snaking its way around the place like a bad smell. The establishment are under scrutiny like never before. We all get that. But the idea that Comrade Jones and his angry mob have the monopoly on being a bit pissed off about this is madness. Did you ever meet anyone who *liked* a dodgy banker or a thieving MP? But let's not get too bogged down with such minor details. As political narratives have shifted, Owen has become the media's appointed poster boy for left-wing thinking. Stockport's own Citizen Smith. But there's a bit of a problem.

Owen is from privileged stock. He grew up in a middle-class family with professional parents and a nice house in leafy Cheshire. He went to Oxford University. Yet despite this advantageous background, Jonesy has, unfathomably, become the go-to man for all things working class – the default booking on all matters related to the plight of the proletariat. A subject he has not a scintilla of personal experience in. Doesn't even *he* find that a bit odd?

The class issue is a bit like the issue of race: you need to have lived it to hold any kind of authentic view. You can theorise, empathise and even make some vague intellectual leaps into the discussion. But you will never *feel* it. You'll never *really* know. Yet when Owen isn't dreaming about how Labour are about to morph into a contemporary version of the Marxist Party, this has become his métier. The conversation in news rooms must be quite something...

Producer: We need someone to talk about the working classes.

Researcher: What about Owen Jones?

Producer: The middle-class guy who went to Oxford?

Researcher: Yeah, that's him.

Producer: Sounds perfect, book him!

What in the name of Michael Foot's donkey jacket is going on?

It seems the lure of those angry, baggy jumpers, a cuddly northern accent that would rival Alan Bennett's and the added bonus that he doesn't look like Arthur Scargill (oh, and he once wrote a book that most people never read where he interviewed some poor people), is enough for clumsy (and usually southern) media bods to consider Owen the real deal when it comes to the quandary of class.

Even his more recent diatribes bemoaning that the rich are getting richer (ignoring the fact that OJ himself is part of a small and select group of people who has seen his own personal wealth sky-rocket in the past few years; Owen *is* part of the rich) – isn't enough for his conglomerate of left-wing fluffers to take a deep breath and muse a little. The mass media's ignoring of the working classes is almost at criminal levels and sticking Jonesy on the telly every half-hour does nothing to arrest this issue. Where the hell is White Dee when you need her?

11.

THE MIDDLE-CLASS INTELLIGENTSIA

To be fair, OJ isn't the only scribe to darken our doorsteps in the name of class and inequality. The roll-call is quite something.

There's the privately and Oxbridge-educated Laurie Penny (who makes Owen sound like a Thatcherite). Laurie was recently voted one of the '100 People who Matter' by *Tatler* magazine (have the people at *Tatler* never met another human? And what the hell do you have to do to be categorised as *mattering*?) There's the privately and Oxbridge-educated and plagiarising dodge merchant Johann Hari. This halfwit got *so* damn angry about global injustices that he decided to simply make shit up in the name of investigative journalism. Fortunately, he was rumbled, forced to hand back his prestigious Orwell Award and fired from his newspaper. Then there's the privately and Oxbridge-educated, multiple home-owning dynastic queen of the whole damn crew, Polly Toynbee. Poor old Polly can't even raise her feet out of bed in the morning unless she thinks there's an agenda of iniquity to delve into.

Before the Notting Hill mafia start to sniff blood, I get it. We can have all have conversions and epiphanies. The rich and the privileged are as entitled to theirs as anyone else. Just because you live a life of opulence and your own personal experience of social villainy is zero, doesn't mean that you're totally disbarred from the debate. But when that volte-face takes place on such a colossal scale, we're also entitled to smell a big fat rat. Are all of these people really philosophically driven solely by the narrative of injustice? Are they genuinely troubled by what they see as a widening gap between the haves and the have-nots, and an intrinsic desire to redress the balance?

Of course not: their whole charade is bollocks. If you're homeless right now, try knocking on Polly's door and asking if you can have a bed for the night. The butler will have you ejected before you get past the first gargoyle.

Polly & Co. are part of that curious contingent of oddballs who never quite left the teen rebellion stage. The professional anti-establishment gobshites whose continual need to appear virtuous (in public) is like the addict's thirst for the next wrap. Whatever their background or, most worrying, their current circumstances, waving that flag of injustice is what pays their mortgages (if any of them actually had mortgages). Bugger the multifarious contradictions in their own lives, these guys are on a quest to show the rest of us how they intend to right the wrongs of the chronically disadvantaged. Despite years of watching this lot in action, I'm still not sure if this is all deeply sinister or just bloody hilarious.

Seumas Milne is also very much on the list. Milne is Jeremy Corbyn's right-hand man. He's the fuel and the fire behind Brand Corbyn. Very little happens in the life of Jeremy without Milne giving it the green light first. He's also a Marxist journalist of some note. Yet when it comes to his own background,

Seumas Milne makes David Cameron look like a scuzzy street urchin. You would be seriously hard pushed to find a person in journalism and politics more affluent than our Seumas. From the cost of his education, which could solve the national debt of Chad, his inevitable Oxbridge journey, through to his million-pound bank balance, Seumas really is the don of establishment privilege. If I was a Corbyn supporter I would be more than a tad devastated that the person in charge of fighting off the Conservatives and their alleged attachment to wealth was this man.

The debate surrounding social mobility in this country is a constant on the news agenda. How do we address the poverty of education that exists in so many parts of our country? What is the best way to break those establishment networks that currently dominate public life so as to give ordinary kids a fighting chance? The current cast of characters claiming to advance these arguments is beyond farcical.

Seumas Milne sent his own kids to the very best grammar schools in the country, despite being philosophically against their very existence. He is also the man who writes directives for Jeremy about why grammars are the worst thing to happen to the human race since the bubonic plague. Similarly, Polly Toynbee sent her children to hugely expensive private schools while firing off her weekly columns on extravagance and in-equality from her million-pound villa in Tuscany. This dozy pair, along with a handful of privileged others, are pretty much the UK's default voices on social mobility.

If the government ever did decide to take the social mobil-ity issue seriously and advertise for a Class Tsar – someone whose authentic background, experience and lived-through qualifications might make a real difference to this national disaster – one thing is absolutely for sure: the quartet that is Laurie, Johann, Polly and Seumas would be laughed out of the interview room before they'd even sat down.

12.

JERRY THE DOWNLOAD FIEND

Buried deep in the east side of the Paryaqaqa Mountains of southern Peru lives a very powerful man. A man with such unparalleled responsibility that even world leaders are not allowed to know his exact location or identity. We'll call him Jerry.

Jerry is in charge of all things G related. That's G as in 3, or 4. He's also the supreme commander of the world's Wi-Fi networks. From speed to availability, signal strength to download potential, Jerry holds the impressive responsibility of controlling the success of every phone and tablet on earth. Armed with a large brain, a network of super-computers and a massive red joystick, Jerry whiles away the hours fine-tuning, increasing and reducing, stopping and starting the way us Westerners receive our 4G and Wi-Fi. Not to put too fine a point on it, when it comes to matters tech, Jerry very much controls the fluency of all of our lives. Nobody can truly say how Big J was appointed (we can never be allowed to know) but his clandestine existence is clearly paramount to the dis-combobulation of the human race. I'm told that there has only been one *possible* sighting of the man in twenty years (many got close but paid the price, perhaps) and any communication he does make comes via the conduit of a small mountain goat called Victor.

I appreciate that all of this does sound a bit David Icke (Alex Jones for American readers), but hear me out. If we didn't believe in Jerry and his mischievous global mission, our only other option is to think the unthinkable: that every telecom company, service provider and supplier of wireless technology has been bullshitting us for years about the *actual* capabilities of their networks. This of course would be a preposterous notion, an awful way to think of some of the UK's best-loved tech corporations. So until I hear to the contrary, Jerry has to exist.

•   •   •

I'm on a train to Manchester. My phone tells me I have 4G. I couldn't be happier (remember those crap old days of 3G? Well, here I am with a very healthy 4). Time to get busy. But hang on. I'm halfway through writing an email and the damn thing has disappeared on me. Where did it go? The train hasn't even moved and my 4G has legged it. I stare at my screen, confused. I take evasive action. Lob it into airplane mode and switch it back on again (the equivalent of rolling the batteries in the back of a remote control). I wait. It flickers. Get in there, it's back ... oh, hang on, it's gone again. Now it says 3G; that'll be fine. I can work with the old 3, not as fast but who cares. My email suggests it's sending (not sent, just sending). Five minutes pass. It's still sending. After thirty seconds the 3G has vanished, and so has my email – consigned to drafts. As our train begins to move, I take some unqualified comfort in the fact that this signal issue is merely a blip and by the time we start moving it's bound to come back. And it does. From time to time.

By the time we reach Milton Keynes, my phone is unequivocal: the 4G has returned. It's even loaded the Google homepage; this must be a good sign. I decided to go for a drop of social media. I hit my Facebook app and wait. And wait some more. Facebook is clearly a trickier beast than the Google page. It doesn't want to play ball. But it *says* I have a full-blown 4G signal. Why will it not load? I revert to airplane mode. I then cautiously slide the phone back into action. But there is no 4G. There never was, of course. Someone or something is telling me a huge pack of lies. An hour into my journey and things are grim. I have sent one email, listened to half a song and have partially read a few tweets before the big blue bird gave up the ghost. My sighs and grunts are clearly audible. The man in the seat in front keeps doing that over-the-shoulder look thing. He's either annoyed or concerned. I meet his gaze but he just grins at me, like he's come face to face with an alien. My frustrations continue for another forty minutes.

It was then that I saw the Messiah. Not *the* Messiah, of course (baby Jesus would surely be in first class anyway) but a messianic message of pure love. My saviour had come to get me. The sign couldn't have been clearer: FREE WI-FI AVAILABLE ON THIS TRAIN. Thank you, God. Thank you. And screw you, 4G, I'm off with the big boys. The world of train-based Wi-Fi is calling me and I'm about to sign up to the mission.

Turns out it wasn't free at all (unless you were with Jesus in first class) but a fiver is mere bagatelle in order to get my sanity back. I spend the obligatory ten minutes signing my life away in order to become part of the Wi-Fi family. Bingo. I'm in. Sod my crock of half-written emails and posts, I have ninety minutes of the journey left and I'm going to enjoy it. Bring on the iPlayer. *Koko: the Gorilla Who Talks to People*, I'm told, is a must-watch documentary. I can't think of a more ambient time to sit down and enjoy the antics of a talking monkey than relaxing on a train.

Unfortunately, Koko isn't talking very much. At least not to me. I'm getting nothing. Just a frozen screen that shows a slightly blurred image of a massive ape siting in a kitchen. Every few minutes, the image moves. I'm now looking at Koko pointing to a pie chart. This is surely gripping stuff but it ain't really happening. I've been scuppered, again – seduced into the cult of Wi-Fi and paid back with nothing more than disappointment and grief. Koko is now stroking a kitten. But it's all too late. My relationship with this beast is over before it's started. My screen is having none of it.

The train guard is checking tickets. I decide to dive in and ask what the frick is going on. It's a simple and swift conversation.

'Excuse me, is there a reason why the Wi-Fi isn't working?' I ask.

'Should be OK. What are you trying to do?' he says, helpfully.

'Well, I'm trying to watch a documentary about a talking monkey on the iPlay-...'

'Let me stop you there, sir. The Wi-Fi is really for checking email and stuff but it won't work for much more than that. iPlayer and films are pretty much a no-no.'

How the hell does that work? I'm on a train that brags (and

sells) a Wi-Fi service – the spirit of that statement suggests that one might actually be able to use it.

'Anyone else ever mentioned this before?' I enquire.

'Yeah, everyone,' he says, before scuttling off. Who says customer service is dead?

I arrive at Manchester Piccadilly exhausted. I want to cry. In three hours I've written eight emails (all sitting in my drafts folder), several Facebook messages that I can't post, and I've managed to watch seven minutes of a sixty-minute monkey documentary. My day was never meant to be like this. Eventually, I connected to a 3G signal and watched my messages glide from their respective boxes and out to their various recipients.

My mate Will (a tech journalist of some standing) tried to reassure me that this experience was exceptional because I was on a train. I had countered his weak theory by pointing out that this was also the twenty-first century and, train or not, this shit really should work by now. In any case, it isn't that exceptional. We are all regularly deceived and infuriated by weak or non-existent G and Wi-Fi signals. Even when our phones are telling us otherwise. Quite how multifarious suppliers of such services get away with flogging you something that is at best shaky and at worst total rubbish remains one of life's great corporate mysteries.

●　　●　　●

In the past couple of years, Jerry has been handed a new project. He is now CEO and sole supplier of all deals relating to super-fast broadband. I'm told that when he got the contract, him and Victor laughed so hard that ancient rocks were seen falling from the Peruvian mountainside forming a perfectly sculptured middle finger upon landing.

I also still have no idea whether or not Koko really can talk. I suspect not.

13.

REALITY TV MORONS

Including reality TV people in the big 67 was always going to be a close call. It's a bit of an open goal. But given where we've ended up in the world of popular culture, it would surely be the mother of all failures not to have a little poke into the upside-down world of what now passes for celebrity.

Take that fella Rylan. He was the guy who came about fifth on *The X Factor* after Louis & Co. finally decided that he wasn't that good (most of us had worked this out about sixteen weeks earlier). But Ry wasn't about to take such a public lashing on the chin. Diligently, he took evasive action: he painted his hair black, sprayed his face orange, had a nag's worth of teeth implanted into his head and became a TV presenter. What else?

Lobbing a reality 'star' into the dizzy world of TV presentation is now pretty de rigueur and our man Ry is merely one of many to subjugate the domain previously (and sacredly) occupied by the likes of Edmonds, Ball or Evans. Times change, I guess, but it's pretty much impossible to imagine that such an accelerated move could happen with any other profession. To compound the confusion, it turns out that those who first came to prominence via ridicule and vulgarity actually go on to earn a pretty impressive living from it.

Rylan Clark is now one of the main hosts of those mini versions of *Big Brother/X Factor* shows. He's also a regular on the daytime TV circuit, dispensing his showbiz wisdom for the baying crowds. He's just the latest to have trodden that well-worn path of shame into the lucrative world of the telly. In order to bag an impressive gig (post-mass national humiliation) you *might* have imagined that the big cheeses in TV land would need to first have a slightly uncomfortable conversation...

'Look, Reality Person, you've never done this job in your life and so the chances are you won't be very good at it; in fact, you'll probably be more than a bit ropey, so we're going to pay you £250 a week and if it works out we'll raise it to £350 for the next series.'

That doesn't happen. This happens.

'Look Reality Person, you've never done this job in your life and so the chances are you won't be very good at it; in fact, you'll probably be more than a bit ropey, so we're going to pay you £100,000 for the first series and we'll raise it to £125k for the next.'

Buggeration! Is there any other job on the planet where someone would actively desire to pay you a bucket-load of money (that you hadn't even asked for) based on zilch experience and the upfront acknowledgement that you won't be very good at it?

To poke this conundrum further, most of the Reality Massive are so hungry for a drop of fame, they'd happily do the job for sod all. Twelve weeks earlier they'd been working in

Currys on minimum wage; they're hardly likely to go all Alan Sugar at the negotiating table.

So what should be the mother of all of weaknesses (they're a bit shit) curiously becomes their greatest strength and, disturbingly, that's the whole point. If you ask the Rylanettes what they love about their reality hero, they're likely to tell you that his total lack of experience and inability to gob out a coherent sentence is central to the attraction. On that basis, my nan could be fronting half these shows, but let's not over-analyse.

My mate Laura says I'm missing the point. Then again, this is the girl who thinks that *Geordie Shore* should have won a BAFTA for best documentary. Her contention is that all this guff is just a new and emerging genre of TV that isn't meant to be taken seriously. On her advice I had watched an episode of *GS*, just to make sure I wasn't missing out. It went something like this: girl goes out, gets utterly hammered, meets a guy, asks him if he fancies a shag and takes him home. Action then cuts to the house...

'I couldn't shag a lad unless he 'as a six-pack,' says the girl as she drags a drunken Geordie off into the bedroom.

Blimey. This must be the part where they cut to a commercial break. But they don't. Surely they're not going to show ... hang on, yes they are. They're going to show the whole damn thing! It's actually happening – on my own flatscreen. How did we arrive here? This girl is on camera doing the horizontal hula with a fella she's known for three minutes, all in exchange for a bit of fame. What the hell would her mum and dad make of it all? I didn't have to wait long for an answer. Within moments, and against all anthropological odds, up popped the folks.

'*She's a right party girl, our lass, eh?*' says the beaming dad. Turns out, he doesn't just approve of it, he's part of it – all in the name of fifteen minutes on the box. Nice.

So Laura's advice was pants, almost literally. Like all the others, this was a horror show; TV made from the entrails of a thousand demons, and I reserve the right to hate every vacuous and shite-ridden moment. It wasn't so many years ago that Benny Hill was taken off TV despite being watched by a jaw-dropping 23 million viewers each week. The powers that be had correctly identified that it had run its course. The smut-fest was over and titillating telly that dealt in the currency of bare arses and innuendo was a thing of the past – no longer required in a brave, new, progressive world. What the hell happened?

Today, as the dons of the networks continue to play trash-poker with the schedules, the *real* reality is that this once cult-based genre of global telly is fast becoming the mainstream – and that should give anyone the hump. I appreciate that Rylan, White Dee, Charlotte, Dom and Steph are not exactly presenting *Newsnight* (yet) but you'd have to have the brain of a lobotomised chimpanzee not to notice how culturally screwed up we've become when Richard Dawkins commands fewer people at his book signing than Gemma from *Towie* does at hers.

14.

CROWD FUNDERS

It's a beautiful thing. Come up with an idea or plan to make yourself rich and then get other people to pay for it. Genius. I've no idea who first stumbled upon this almost criminal concept and I still can't quite fathom if they are more Charles Ponzi or Bill Gates. Maybe somewhere in between. Either way, the notion of getting someone else to stump up the wonga for your idea or business plan takes audacity into some very new terrain. Right now, across the globe, many thousands of razor-sharp brains are attempting to trouser *your* cash in order to further *their* ambitions. In the real world, this would be called theft. In the heady world of business, it's called being an entrepreneur.

Meanwhile, back in the office, serial entrepreneur Rufus is cooking up his latest plans. After a tense meeting with his two business colleagues, he's come to a decision. He takes a deep breath, fiddles a bit more with his Bic and reclines back into his big chair. Then, like a man about to announce who is going to play the next James Bond, he comes out with it: 'We're gonna go for a crowd funder.' Silence in the room. Then smiles. Trebles all round. Wow, this Rufus bloke knows his beans.

Rufus isn't quite the famed Nigerian prince or the bloke who sold Brooklyn Bridge to tourists, but he's kind of in that ballpark. He's masterminded a way to extract other people's money and create a potential fortune for himself. Just half a dozen gullible investors and Rufus will be sitting pretty.

So, what do you get for contributing to Rufus's pension? The short answer is sod all. This is about the honour of being *involved*, the kudos of being there when the magic happened. Sure, there are some heady projects out there that may well promise you a tiny return on your investment, but all too often these ventures simply rely on you wanting to be part of a business journey that may or may not – statistically the latter – succeed.

More galling is that many of these 'proposals' aren't businesses at all, but pet projects or recreational activities that the chronically vain can't afford to finance themselves. Instead, they go cap in hand to others with spectacular stories of their latest enterprise. As a reward for your financial efforts, you are bestowed with the accolade of being 'thanked' in dispatches. Whoop-dee-doo. So while you sit there staring at your overdrawn bank statement, Rufus Funkwarbler is lying on a hammock in Barbados counting the cash – *your* cash.

15.

NAME BOTHERERS

What was actually going on chez Cumberbatch when the folks decided that the best name for their new-born nipper was Benedict? Was it a bet? Was there some kind of compelling monastic connection? Were they just larking around after a giddy night out at *The National*? Just what *was* going on? They could have called him Terry. *Terry* Cumberbatch. A sort of offsetting of the unusual with something more mainstream. Instead, they decided to just go posh. And annoying. Benedict Cumberbatch is a very annoying name. There's no way around it. If you went to school with anyone with a name like that, it would be a talking point for the entire year – you might as well just stick a giant plastic penis on the kid's head and have done with it.

Another victim whose ancestors were clearly sniffing glue when the names were being dished out is the writer and historian Simon Sebag Montefiore (yes, that *is* a name). Shouldn't you be in jail for saddling a bairn with that kind of ridiculous appellation? Where were the social services? These names are clearly chosen with the specific intention of making a statement, that's kind of the point; it's what the gentry *do*. So it follows that the rest of us are entitled to make a judgement. Forget any reasoned rules of subjectivity, it's an irrefutable fact that some names are just very irritating.

Parodying the posh and their daft names comes as naturally as breathing. The world of comedy has been at it for years: Bubbles DeVere, Mr Cholmondley-Warner etc. Our inner class warriors can't help it. Ben and Si were both educated at the same multi-zillion-pound-a-term private school, a school where no one has even heard of anyone called Terry. For these guys, having a bonkers name compounds the pecking order. For us proles, it's a unique opportunity to mark out our own status via the intellectual conduit of taking the piss.

But this proclivity for daft, and often unpronounceable, names has now gone well beyond the higher echelons of the privileged classes. Today, quirking up your kid's moniker has become as fashionable as owning the latest smartphone. Once upon a time it was de rigueur to select a name that allowed your kid to fit in. Now, it's all about finding one that makes them stand out.

We've all found ourselves in that awkward scenario where your mate announces the name of their cuddly new-born and you have to simply nod politely at the creative nature of their choice.

'We're calling him Barnstable…'

Don't say a word. Don't ever cross that line. It'll cost you a life-long friendship. Insult their choice of car, even mock that decision to paint their hallway Mikado Yellow, or get really brave and finally tell them about that personal freshness issue they've had for years. Just don't ever question or deride their choice of name for their new kid.

But there's another batch of name criminals out there who also deserve some public exposure. This lot really are bat-shit crazy.

I once met a girl called Rowena.

'Hi Rowena, nice to meet you,' I said, offering my hand.

'Er, can we get this out of the way right now, please. It's not Rowena (as in henna), it's Rowena (as in hyena).'

She looked more than a tad miffed, like I was about the twelfth person she'd had to correct that day.

'I'm sorry, I once knew someone with the same name and it was pronounced Rowena, so I assumed...'

'...Well, it isn't and you're about the twelfth person today that I've had to correct. Anyway, how are you?'

Cripes. If I really was the twelfth person that day – and this was a pattern – that's eighty-four times a week that she has the same conversation! Four thousand, three hundred and sixty-eight times a year. This is insane (349,440 over an average lifetime, number fans). Does she really spend all day correcting folk for correctly pronouncing a name that she has chosen to pronounce in a different way? Save yourself the hassle, Ro – just change your name.

Batty Rowena is not alone. There's a proliferation of these self-righteous goofballs who, in a desperate attempt to claim some sort of originality for their standard or banal names, have chosen to go down the counterintuitive pronunciation route in order to give it some added shine. Here's the official top six:

- Karen/K*air*en
- Michaela/Mich*eye*la

- Tania/T*ar*nia
- Jeffery/J*offr*ey
- Aaron/*Air*on
- Ralph/Raif (it could never *ever* be Raif)

The most chronic case I stumbled across came from the usually sane location of New Zealand. A media bod called Natasha had emphatically informed her colleagues that she would go to HR if anyone refused to pronounce her name 'correctly'. She had insisted on being called Nata-Shar (*head hits desk*). This clearly borders on something close to insanity.

If you happen to be one of the above, just take it on the chin. Your name is going to be pronounced however the hell a person wants to. The fact that your folks decreed on day one that they would usurp convention and give your standard moniker a bit more of a romantic vibe is of no interest to me. Or anyone else. You have a dual pronounceable name and because of that you totally relinquish any right to *insist* on how it's enunciated. So don't be precious, just like the 'scon' *v.* 'scone' argument, this is firmly either/or territory and there's not a damn thing you can do about it.

16.

MAN SPREADERS

Trains are a pretty rich territory for people doing barmy things. From that unfathomable bod who sits right next to you despite it being a totally empty carriage (what *is* their thought process?) to the cretin who thinks nothing of opening all the windows (despite it not being hot) thus giving the people two seats away a tornado-style battering for the rest of their journey. You tend not to drive down a motorway at 70mph with all of your windows down, so why do it on a damn train?

And then there's this lot.

For the unenlightened, man spread is the ability to sit with your legs so wide apart you could park a Ford Fiesta between them. This is, as the name suggests, an act usually (although, oddly, not exclusively) undertaken by men. Man spread.

If you've ever tried to spread your legs as wide as you possibly can (give it a go), you'll know just how darn difficult it is. It's also painful. It doesn't – and can't – happen by accident; it's an intended act. The adductor magnus muscle is simply not designed to allow for this kind of leg-based choreography. Legs don't naturally default to that position when you sit down. So what the hell is going on when thousands of men, every day, sit on trains and buses and deliberately decide that their optimum position will be one where their legs are in two different postcodes?

The first time I saw a man spreader, I had, not unreasonably, assumed this was all down to some kind of disability, a prosthetic leg, maybe, that required one to sit in a certain way. Or perhaps it was a delicate inner-thigh rash thing, contracted while bush walking and wearing inappropriate trousers, meaning that spreading the legs was the only way to avoid an inevitable chafing. But, alas, my generous theories were wide of the mark.

My best guess is that this sits somewhere in the sphere of male insecurity. The man spreader is making a public statement, planting a flag in the soil of masculinity and marking his territory for the benefit of his fellow travellers. Like the peacock or the puffer fish, this is about claiming space and dominance: 'Look, I really am a proper man; even my legs do this shit when I sit down.'

Can there be any other explanation?

Unless you're Mr Bendy, the world limb-bending champion, or you happen to be made of pipe-cleaners, this is a very uncomfortable way to sit. There's not a cat in hell's chance that you can do this with any level of ease and without being completely aware of it. Pack it in, you look like an utter arse.

I promise you, man spreaders, if you cross your legs or simply bring them a tad closer together, we won't think you less of a man. So let's be sensible, quit the legs-akimbo lark, stop taking up three seats with your stupid limbs and sit with some damn dignity.

17.

PEOPLE WHO DON'T KNOW HOW TO USE A PHONE

There are a number of crimes going on here.

Let's start with the complete lack of sane protocol when it comes to texting. I promise you, there *is* a way to behave when texting. A set of unwritten regulations that any decent person should be adhering to.

This is a text I sent to my mate Will:

Hi Will. Running a bit late. Do you mind if we meet in the Costa at Leicester Square rather than the one at Holborn? It would make it a bit easier and we wouldn't lose any time?

This is the text he sent back:

K

K? what does he mean, 'K'? I mean, I know what K means: it's an abbreviation of OK. Clearly one of the shortest words in the English language became too much hassle for texting purists and was deemed a bit of a ball-ache, so this was replaced with a simple, time-saving 'K'. But what does *Will* mean by his singular K? Is he annoyed with me?

I texted back:

Are you sure you don't mind? It just makes it easier for time?

He replied:

Sure

Sure? It gets worse. This is no better than OK, or K. He's annoyed. Why is one of my best mates writing back with single words? My changing of the location for our coffee has clearly bugged him. I'm a terrible person for this last-minute alteration to our plans.

When we eventually meet, Will is fine. He hasn't got the hump. Will has simply adopted the next phase in human communication: NCS, or nonchalant conversing syndrome. This *is* a thing. Some of us have only recently calmed down after the great letter purge of 2009, when normal words became misspelt for no good or logical reason. L8R, UR, ABT2 and GR8 entered the texting lexicon with almost no notice and we all spent the next three years trying to work out what the hell our mates were saying.

It appears we've now moved into the next evolution of textspeak, where writing more than one word is too much of a ballache for a time-dependent nation. Who the hell needs sentences? The invariable upshot is that mates on the receiving end tend to think that their co-texters are in a perpetual state of annoyance. K, sure, yep, yeah, whatevs, dunno etc. simply reek of nonchalance. They convey a state of pissed-offedness on the part of the texter. Humans tend not converse monosyllabically in real life to avoid the rest of us thinking they're miserable gits. So how about applying a bit of that logic to texting? This way we can save textees everywhere from thinking that their best mates hate them.

And then there's this lot.

If I send you a text, please don't then *call* me back. The reason I sent you the text is because I wanted to text you, not talk to you. It's possible that later on I might wish to talk but right now the whole point of texting was because it was a desired alternative to talking. Phoning me back is a serious no-no. The likelihood is that I'm not in a position to talk. I might be on a train or in a meeting. Or about to go to the loo. Or *in* the loo. That's why I texted, see. You could text me back and *ask* if I'm free to talk – that's fine. Just don't presume. A text is a text, a call is a call; please do not cross-contaminate the two.

And what's the deal with people who can't understand the concept of a voicemail? If I leave you a voice message, please do what the gods of networks designed it for, and actually listen to it. That way we can avoid this kind of nonsense:

'Hello Mike, Collins here. Please don't call me back yet as I'm about to go into the dentist...'

Two seconds later Mike calls me back.

'Did you not get my voicemail?'

'Yeah, didn't bother to listen to it, easier just to call you back.'

'But the voicemail said don't call me back.'

'Right, I didn't hear it.'

'I know, you just told me that.'

Easier to call me back? Clearly not. I promise you, I'm not making stuff up here: the whole damn purpose of leaving a voicemail is for the person at the other end to actually listen to it. By definition, it contains some information that I want you to hear.

Headphones crimes have also reached unacceptable levels. Where is the UN when you need them? Every other person I pass in the street seems to be making the same fundamental mistake. Years back, a very clever person in a very impressive phone laboratory designed a set of headphones that double up as a cable for talking on the phone. It's all rather simple. You stick one bit in your ear (or ears) and halfway down the lead is a little microphone which picks up your voice. You can then stick the phone in your pocket and talk away to your chums. What you don't need to do is hold the phone up to your mouth. The phone is no longer acting as a mouthpiece once you have plugged the cable in; the cable cancels out the mic on the phone. Talking into the phone is doing nothing. It just makes you look a bit weird.

Equally, that very clever phone lab person also designed the little microphone in the cable to pick up your voice from a distance. You don't need to hold it up to your mouth: its entire design is so that you specifically *don't* have to do this. I've seen folk almost eating the damn things, presumably in the name of being heard. Pack it in.

It would also be totally remiss not to mention the Horizontal Phone Monsters. These are the people who, for reasons unknown, have taken to holding their phone in a horizontal position in front of their face when talking into it. This involves contorting your hand to a completely unnatural angle to achieve the aim. I can only assume this is copied behaviour from watching contestants on *The Apprentice* or jubilant families on *The X Factor*. Just to let you into a little trade secret, the only reason telly contestants hold the phone that way is so that they don't cover their face with their own mobiles in front of the TV cameras – they have been asked to do it. It's not a fashion statement or some kind of telephonic optimum way to talk; it's about camera angles for the telly. Nothing more. So try to avoid giving yourself carpal tunnel syndrome and hold the damn phone right up to ya lughole.

18.

AUDIENCE PARTICIPATION LOONS

If ever there was a phrase likely to induce me to leg it, Mo Farah-style, from any kind of function, it's when the guest host utters that *Turn to the person next to you and give them a big hug* thing. What the hell? I'm on a grown-up night out, not at a fricking pantomime. And I don't even know the person next to me (yes, I know that's the point) so why would I wish to hug them? They are no doubt feeling the same. And how do you momentarily hug a stranger? Do you go both arms? One arm? Is it a cheek-to-cheek affair or head-over-the-shoulders number? Whatever the protocol, the upshot is a slightly miffed audience thinking that it might just have been better had we not done that in the first place.

Myself and my mate Laura recently went to a charity comedy night (strictly one glass of free Prosecco and some B-list celebs thrown in) where the guest compère took this wanky idea a step further: *Turn to the person next to you and give them a kiss on the lips*. I was standing by a wall with no one on my left but Laura to my right. As mates, there was an immediate mutual look of *sod that*. Unfortunately, standing next to Laura was David Mellor. Mellor appeared to be puckering up for the kill.

Laura was gone so fast I hardly saw it happen. Like one of those magicians who disappear under a cloak on stage and then reappear in the audience two seconds later. Impressive stuff. Unfortunately, this left *me* standing next to David Mellor. Every sinew of my metrosexual being was called to action. Mellor looked me up and down like I was some cheap Parisian whore. Clearly I wasn't his type. His assessment turned to clear disgust – this relationship was going nowhere.

Meanwhile Laura was getting in the pints, looking victorious. She'd dodged a grim bullet. And so had I. But why were we (and 200 others) put in this excruciating position in the first place? What's the gain? Where's the gag? The upshot is only ever humiliating discomfort. The low laughs and clunky mumbles that follow are a pretty clear testament to the collective unease.

There was probably a time – the heady days of Jimmy Cricket, maybe – when this kind of pooled hilarity was a bit funny. Dragging folk up on stage, the weird and almost mandatory *Are you having a good time?* question (nearly always met with an unenthusiastic *Yeeeeah*, which only serves to encourage the same question to be asked again with added zing) and impromptu sing-a-longs etc. would have made for a cracking night out. That agonising charade of *Everybody clap your hands*, which begins with an entire crowd dutifully obliging but quickly descends into a half-arsed hand-slapping thing before full-blown nonchalance sets in (aside from two characters at the back, still at it) must have felt like one of life's social highlights. But we've evolved and our communal palettes need a tad more than this kind of humiliating tripe. I think I speak for the entire human race when I politely ask every comic, after-dinner speaker and host to quit this kind of shit and just get on with the funny stuff.

19.

OVER-35S AT MUSIC FESTIVALS

Apparently, when you have a car crash, the brain does something amazing. It forgets the trauma and blanks out the really bad bits. It's a safety mechanism designed to arrest post-traumatic stress from being any more damaging than it might otherwise be. A similar neurological feat also happens to anyone over the age of thirty-five who still thinks it's acceptable to go to music festivals.

The festival scene is the domain of the young. Three days living like a mucky caveman when you are eighteen is about as good as it gets. When you hit your mid-thirties, it's an affront to everything you would normally stand for. Yet year after year this weirdo subset dutifully jump online to sign up for Knob Fest 2017. And all that goes with it.

'… *But Peabo Bryson is doing an acoustic set on the Fairweather-Lowe Stage … It's a must-see.*'

Oh, do belt up. You've been at it for years and for much of that time it was fun. But now it's time to quit. Sure, you've got a blurry photo of Kanye under those fluorescent lights taken from three miles away while perched on the almost arthritic shoulders of your partner, and a vague memory of seeing Dolly and Bruce give it large on the Pyramid stage. But what about the rest of it?

What your brain has forgotten is just how much you hated all the bits in between (which is most of the festival): the queues, the potent whiff of hippy, the even stronger aroma of Class Bs (which you can no longer touch because you gave up smoking eight years ago in favour of yoga), the wet sleeping bag, the theft of your wallet, that drunk bloke who took a pee on your rucksack, the party of seventeen who held an impromptu rave just outside your two-man bivouac, the fact that attending to your ablutions means dousing yourself in half a litre of Evian and taking a poop involves searching for a bush or a bucket rather than a bona fide bog.

Then there's the hot dog that will set you back about £27 (and the queue to get it will take three hours), the stage that's six miles from where you pitched the tent, the awkward stares from fellow festivalites (who are two decades younger than you) wondering why a granddad is attending *their* gig, and the incontrovertible fact that you and your other half *will* row because despite the kudos you believe this mini-weekender has brought you, you both secretly know that it was a very bad idea and you'd much rather be back home in your local pub with other mid-thirties mates discussing whether or not baby Nazareth will get a place at your preferred nursery.

All of these things will be miraculously erased from your mind as you upload several hundred fuzzy pics of your musical idols onto that rarely looked-at Instagram account…

'… *Look, can you see him, on the right, next to the speaker, that's Peabo.*'

The uncomfortable reality is that you didn't *really* want to go in the first place. You just thought you did. You were in love with the idea, the stories, those endless photos and the vague reassurance that you are still a little bit cool. You paid £250 for this filth-ridden experience and your treasured memories probably added up to no more than about twelve minutes. Time to leave it alone, don't you think?

It's also worth bearing in mind that shedloads of irresponsible young people would rather you weren't there either – it's *their* party. Not yours. So bugger off and keep your mid-thirties weekends for what they are meant to be for: school fêtes, red wine and a healthy dose of *Strictly*.

20.

THATCHER LOVERS

Margaret Thatcher was not the Messiah. Nor was she a genius. She didn't invent capitalism, nor did she conceive the notion of personal responsibility. Thatcher's arrival into Downing Street came with the most monumental piece of political serendipity our country has ever seen. In short, she lucked in. For the Thatcherettes who still follow their leader with a mysterious, cult-like, reverence, there are some inconvenient truths.

The 1970s were grim, with neither the Tories nor Labour being able to make any kind of convincing case for stable government. From three-day weeks and inflation at 30 per cent to nightly blackouts and the inability to bury our dead (due to totally unreasonable public sector workers asking to be paid actual money for their labour), the nation was in a state of advanced decay.

While the 1950s had signified a kind of post-war euphoria, and the '60s some heady liberation from statist conformity, the '70s became the decade that saw a rudderless nation cocooned in a bubble of shit. There was very little to celebrate about this missing decade. Culture purists will cite the Curly Wurly and *Star Wars* as reasons to be cheerful; it's a nice try but I'll raise you an Austin Allegro and Blue Nun – no contest. Other than the emergence of David Bowie, there were few positives to perm from the 1970s. With a similar malaise infesting our political system, it was safe to say that a syphilitic chimpanzee could have got themselves elected as Prime Minister if they made the right noises.

Thatcher never denied that her gender played a part. In 1979, there were just nineteen female MPs in the entire system. Being female was indeed a USP in itself. Thatcher revelled in this status despite her subsequent resistance to all matters feminist. Her background also made her unique within her own party, which back then was still very much dominated by aristocratic, land-owning patriarchs who were so posh they could hardly talk. These men saw Maggie as a bit of a joke, an upstart, even. After Heath, the son of a brickie, they now had Thatch, the daughter of a grocer – what the hell had happened to their party? Still, the nation was in a mess, so why not give the female commoner the poisoned chalice and then re-group in a few years?

Just a few decades or so earlier and Thatcher's gender and class would have been enough to pretty much disqualify her from even being a member of the Tory Party. By 1979, it was these very attributes that took her to ruling the country. No in-depth political philosophy was required. All she had to do was turn up. It was perception, not policy, that catapulted Mrs T into No. 10. Thatcher had won a political lottery.

Not long into her first term in office, along came Ronald Reagan. Reaganomics was not the work of a slightly dim former Hollywood idol but of the wider machine on Capitol

Hill. As America accelerated its capitalist approach to the globe, Thatcher – along with all other Western leaders – dutifully signed up to the project. This was the political equivalent of copying your mate's homework.

It's a little-known fact that the right to buy your council house was well under way *before* Thatcher was even party leader. Even under the Labour government, social housing was being flogged off – Labour had proposed the idea as far back as the 1950s. By the time Thatcher came into power, tens of thousands were already sitting pretty in homes formerly owned by the taxpayer. Thatcher spotted the huge potential and, in a Milli Vanilli-like duping of the nation, simply nicked the idea as her own.

And then came the invasion of the Falklands. Never has a Tory been so grateful for a bunch of foreigners nicking stuff. Thatcher revelled in this and took no time at all in sending in the boys. A few missiles later and some patriotic speeches at the dispatch box and the job was done. Thatcher walked the next election and every die-hard Tory convinced himself that Mrs T had the moral compass of Desmond Tutu.

If you were a woman in a man's world back in the early '80s, the only way was up. Thatcher needed a new war. In Maggie's world, if you woke up in the morning and there was no sign of gyp on the horizon, you pretty much concluded that Armageddon must be around the corner. The unions had been in a thorn in the side of all previous governments. No leader had managed to successfully negotiate their way to harmony. Maggie came up with a cunning plan. The socialist Prime Minister Harold Wilson had begun the process of closing coal mines. Why not continue this but palm it off as your own idea and simultaneously curb the dominance of unreasonable unions? The magpie had struck again and 115 coal mines were earmarked for closure. As for actually negotiating with union bosses, that kind of went by the wayside. Instead, she just shouted at them. Very loudly. And then crushed them.

If you cast your eye over the tick list of Thatcher's greatest achievements, you would be hard pushed to argue that most of these things wouldn't have happened anyway. Do we seriously believe that had Mr and Mrs Roberts not hatched a Margaret back in 1925, we would be sitting here today in a country that had yet to discover homeownership and entrepreneurialism? Would the dead still be unburied and the lights constantly off?

Some things are just part of a bigger cycle and are at the mercy of global considerations as well as domestic. Whichever leader happens to be holding the baton when the story flips takes either the rap or the glory. I have no doubt that if you're a Tory then you really do believe that Mrs T's CV of change and achievement speaks for itself. But to suggest all her feats occurred because of some philosophically engineered magic beans that she sprinkled onto a sick nation is cobblers. Just don't tell the Thatcherettes: it makes them crazy. They literally turn blue and sprout a mad bouffant hairdo before making a pilgrimage up the east coast and burying themselves in a shallow grave in Grantham.

21.

PHOTO WEIRDOS

My mate Del is a tech geek. He spends much of the day engrossed in computer games having pretend wars with people in Japan. He recently completed a particularly hazardous tour of duty in Yawatahama where he single-handedly freed an entire town from what looked like inevitable subjugation by Russian separatists. The visual world is crucial to Del's existence and anyone who has ever watched him go mental with a joystick knows just how seriously he takes his time online. When Del isn't shooting up Putin's finest, he sells spanners to the medical profession, an online business he began from his bedroom a decade ago and which now pays him fairly reasonable dividends. Del is the very epitome of what a man who spends too much time on the internet is supposed to look like: bearded, spec-sporting, T-shirt-wearing, slightly portly and a man of *very* few words. Watching the nightly news with Del is something to behold.

Fiona Bruce: And we start with some breaking news. We're getting reports that aliens have taken over the White House and are now running the administration. It's thought that the head of the intergalactic group is now ensconced in the Oval Office and is due to make a statement in the next hour…

Del: (with zero facial movements) Terrible.

To say that Del is an understated type doesn't even get close to describing the laid-back nature of this cuddly tech bunny.

But if you whip out your phone and take a photo of him, something odd happens. Del has a selfie face. I mean a *proper* selfie face. Stoical Del turns into Joe Pasquale. The eyebrows raised, the mouth open, the look of sheer surprise complete. Sometimes he'll even point a finger at the camera for added gusto. If he's in a double shot, he'll avert his eyes towards his co-star in a clear re-working of the *curious look*. How the hell did this happen? How did my super-serious, non-fazed mate Del turn all wacky for the camera?

Del is not alone. I guess the first human foray into the in-explicable world of face posing was the (mostly female) trout pout thing – a wholly unfathomable fad of doing stuff with your lips in order to make yourself look like a bit of a twat (was there ever going to be any other result?). Since then, we've had the *finger on the lip* thing, in what one can only assume was originally intended to be a sensual and seductive look but, given the wide range of folk who did it, turned into anything but. We also have the still active *hand on one hip pose* – a stance once strictly reserved for the world of the supermodel but which has somehow been clumsily hijacked by anyone who fancies trying to replicate the look (includ-ing my auntie Pat, who, with respect, is anything but catwalk material). We now exist in a curious time where saying cheese is no longer good enough to pass the strict rules of being in a photo. If you can't pose properly, you're not part of the gang.

A few years ago we did a piece on the radio about a woman who had taken photograph of herself in her bathroom mirror and hadn't realised that she had left the camera phone *in* the picture. The image went briefly viral as folk across the land didn't discuss her hair or make-up but how this ninny had gone to all that trouble to look good and yet somehow managed to take a shot of herself with her iPhone in full view. How we laughed. I'm not sure if this image was the first of its kind but we all know what has happened since then.

Taking a photo of yourself in your own bathroom mirror has now moved into even more narcissistic territory, as men and women across the world think nothing of whipping off their kit in order to display their impressive bods to the masses. A decade ago we would have been questioning someone's mental health if they did this kind of thing. Today we celebrate and endorse it. Uploading images onto virtual clouds in order to play out our lives on Instagram and Facebook has become an automated part of one's day. If a work colleague suddenly took their clothes off and ran around the office shouting, 'Look at me, guys, check out my toned torso, it's amazing,' you would either kick them in the shins or call the medics. Transpose the same behaviour to the online world and all is fine and dandy. We seriously have to question what has happened to our evolutionary journey when posting teasing images of your barely clothed genitals to the public has become hard-wired into the minds of the many.

I've yet to see any photos of my mate Del posing in front of a mirror in his pants. My fear – my *genuine* fear – is that it can only be a matter of time.

22.

TWITTER NEWS BUNNIES

When you first sign up to Twitter, you have to make the very important life decision about who you want to follow. Clearly, all your mates, your own interest groups, one or two recommendations from friends, and Stephen Fry. If you don't follow Fry then eternal damnation is on the way. It is also a given that, somewhere in there, you'll follow one of the big news outlets, whether it's LBC, the BBC, Sky or CNN. It's reasonable to say that pretty much everyone on Twitter follows at least one news thread.

There are few rules on Twitter: it's pure Mad Max territory and if you plan to analyse the human condition via this particular strand of social media then you'll leave with many more questions than answers. As previously established, some behaviour is worrying, some of it criminal and quite a lot of it insane. But there's also another category, one that doesn't get talked about enough: people who think they are George Alagiah.

Discussing news on Twitter is bread-and-butter stuff. It's kind of the point. *Breaking* the news is a different thing altogether. The moment something hits the official news wires, it's on Twitter within a nanosecond. Every radio and TV station on the planet has fired off the story the moment it arrived. The story is usually pre-tagged with the scary word BREAK-ING and is invariably followed up with a series of supporting tweets covering any developments. Anyone looking at their Twitter feed during this time will see a bombardment of messages all relaying the news. You could be under no illusion as to what has just happened. Which is why I'm a bit confused as to why Lenny in Blackpool (his profile says he's a brickie) also wants to urgently inform the world of the latest story.

Lenny is not a one-off. If you check your Twitter feed during the time of a developing story, you will see myriad of tweeters all vying for a first-past-the-post position on the latest story. I'm unsure if this is a genuine need to impart important news to uninformed followers or just the desire to be first out the traps with the goss. Either way, it's all a bit crackers considering the very people they are telling (their own followers) have pretty much a 100 per cent chance of having seen the story from one of the official news outlets. No amount of speed-typing on your keyboard is likely to beat the Press Association.

Lenny has even adopted the industry style of using the pre-tag BREAKING in front of his tweets and then following them up with 'I'm hearing now…' type phrases to bolster the urgency. I'm asking you nicely, Lenny: stop it. If you were sitting at home watching Jon Snow on *Channel 4 News* giving you the low-down on the grim turn of events in the Middle East and your neighbour suddenly shouted through your letter box, 'Have you seen the news?', you might also think that was a bit odd.

I'm sure Lenny would point out that many of *his* followers

may not have had a chance to catch up on the latest so he's simply letting them know what's happening – not everyone follows news organisations, after all. Fair point but that doesn't stop you doing my nut in, Len. Can't we leave it to CNN to tell us that Donald Trump has just spit roasted a Mexican?

Without sounding like an arse, this whole breaking news thing does take on an even more pronounced vibe when I get these tweets sent to me personally while I'm at work. This even happens while I'm on air.

@IanCollinsUK Ian, have you seen the news on the bombing in Syria?

Yes, I work in a news room.

@IanCollinsUK Ian, have you seen this [link attached] – you might find it helpful. It kind of ties in with what you're talking about.

No, it doesn't tie in. This *is* what we're talking about.

@IanCollinsUK Hey Ian, David Cameron has just resigned.

Yep, spotted that.

I don't want to sound unkind and sometimes people are just being helpful, but it is bloody strange. If I tweeted the manager of B&Q to make sure that she was aware of the sale in the greenhouse department, I'm pretty sure she would have a similar view.

I long ago gave up trying to mentally police the shenanigans on Twitter. It's a fool's errand and if you let it bother you, your brain will eventually shrink to the size of a small pea. That doesn't mean that we don't pass judgement along the way, so if you don't mind, Lenny, I'm blocking you now for crimes of general annoyance.

23.

THATCHER HATERS

For how long can a new government blame the last one for the political or economic failures of the day? If a new government cops a recession within three months of being in office, it's more than reasonable to assume this was down to conditions left by the previous administration. If, after four years, things start to go pear-shaped, then it's a fair assumption the incumbents have got it wrong. This argument has gone on for years, with all sides claiming immunity from blame due to the abject irresponsibility of the last lot. The general consensus seems to be that two years (in normal circumstances) is about where the bar should be set.

Unless you're talking about Margaret Thatcher.

If ever you're lost for a damn good reason as to why life is a bit shit, just blame Thatcher. Despite the fact that it's coming up for half a century since she became leader of the Tories, if you're looking for a convenient way out of any given political debate, citing the 'T' word is your get out of jail free card. Everything can lead back to Mrs T – she's the Mornington Crescent of political discourse.

The abridged version of why Thatcher wasn't just wrong

but *actually* evil goes something like this: she sold off poor people's houses, flogged the phone and the gas companies to some rich people (*all* of whom were apparently her personal besties), took away milk from small children, rewired all of our DNA to make us selfish and culled puppies as a social pastime in the back garden of Downing Street. On top of all of that, she was a woman. And these things are so much worse when carried out by a woman.

Whenever we've run debates on this one (which is often), the suggestion that Thatcher was single-handedly responsible for an entire nation suddenly becoming greedy swine obsessed with money is invariably top of the list. It's more than interesting that the person imparting this cracking piece of wisdom doesn't concede to being greedy themselves. They will also tell you that their parents aren't greedy and nor were their grandparents. In fact, none of their friends are greedy either. Their milkman doesn't appear to be greedy and Bob, who runs their local pub, is a very generous man and anything but greedy. None of Bob's family harbour the greed gene either. Even more interestingly, everyone he knows and everyone they know all dodged the greedy bullet too. The reason for this is that the premise is utter bollocks to begin with. Thatcher could no more make people greedy than she could turn water into wine.

More high-octane BS comes in the form of school milk. Harold Wilson and the previous Labour administration had begun the process of taking milk away from school kids in 1968. Nobody said a word. Under the Tories, the policy continued. Thatcher, being Education Secretary, had to implement the changes. It's a little-known fact (and an inconvenient truth) that when the milk debate found its way to the Cabinet table, the only minister to be against this move was, er, Thatcher. But under the Cabinet collective responsibility rules, she was forced to accept them. She did get one small concession and that was to keep the milk going for the poorest children. Nonetheless, the damage was done. By a beautiful coincidence, her name rhymed with the word snatcher, meaning Mrs T became Thatcher the Milk Snatcher for the rest of time. No such rhythmic chant has ever been applied to Ted Short, the previous Labour Education Secretary, who got rid of milk for every 11–18-year-old in the land. But then Ted was a man and Short has no such appropriate rhyme. Margaret being a female, with real-life breasts and stuff, meant that taking milk from a child became the perfect metaphor for all that was wrong with the wicked Conservatives. To this day, otherwise intelligent adults choose to believe that Mrs T removed school milk for no other reason than she was biologically evil.

There is a bucket-load of reasons to disagree with Thatcherism, but daft lefties constantly seem to revert to these same tired, false or monumentally reimagined arguments. The concept of a greater emphasis on self-reliance and less intervention from the state may well be a notion you disagree with but these things are hardly acts of evil, just a different point of view. In any case, back in the early '80s modern capitalism and the Big Bang were coming our way regardless of who was in No. 10. These changes were happening across the entire planet. I often wonder if German phone-in programmes are bogged down with calls about what an evil old bastard Helmet Kohl was. I doubt it.

Even Blair with his chronically illegal penchant for shooting up Arab folk hasn't managed to usurp the outcry and ridicule reserved for Mrs T. Perhaps it's the comedy hair and the daft voice that does it. Or the fact that it's so much easier to caricature a woman as being thoroughly wicked than a man – popular culture and history will bear that out.

Whatever the reasons, the next time you're debating Brexit, Syria, Trident or the existence of Vernon Kay and the argument isn't going your way, remember – just play the Thatcher card. If nothing else, stupid people will think you know what you're talking about.

24.

PEOPLE WHO CAN'T STOP CLAPPING

THE CINEMA

Just in case any of you are not au fait with how a cinema works, let me explain. That massive screen you are staring at really is just a screen. The people you see on it are not actually there – they are being projected onto the screen via a device called a projector. The projector has been loaded up with a copy of the film which is merely being beamed onto said screen for the enjoyment of the audience. None of the actors who are in the film are actually in the cinema with you; they aren't hiding behind the screen acting out the scenes. Nor are they secretly waiting in the wings while their finest work is being played out. It would clearly be a ridiculous ask of our finest thesps to be present in all cinemas at all times. Even Vinnie Jones isn't that versatile. Which is why there is no need for you to clap like a super-charged moron when the film is over. Like the falling tree in the forest, no one is there to hear you. It's pointless, so pack it in.

My source down at the multiplex tells me that on the big movie releases this spontaneous applause nonsense happens in about one in every eight showings, usually within the first two weeks of a release. After that, for reasons unknown, it stops. He also suggests (and this is not peer-reviewed) that the average clapper tends to be a mid-twenties male with a mad beard and a tatty leather jacket. Cinemas, like most public buildings, have signs telling us not to smoke and not to run in the event of fire. Maybe it's time to add a little extra rule about this clapping lark? This is why pulling out of the EU was a palpably bad idea. If anyone could make a law where you can't imagine one was needed, it's the big cheeses down there at the EU.

EU Directive 1546

Anyone caught clapping at a plastic screen will be seen as an utter nuisance and not conducive to the public good. This will be punishable by a remote-controlled bucket of horse shit tipped onto your head from the cinema gantry.

THE PLANE

I'm reliably informed that this still goes on. I've been on two flights when the clapping thing happened. I'm still confused about what the deal is here. The protocol is quite clear: pilots don't require a spontaneous round of applause just because they landed a plane. They are paid to do exactly that. Landing is not an optional extra – even Ryanair haven't considered charging for it. We don't clap the bus driver when they make a particularly impressive stop at Mayweather Avenue. Folk would stare. Nor do we applaud the man who comes to read your gas meter. 'Oh my God, he's got all four digits in one go – the skill of this man is extraordinary. Give him a round of applause.'

So what's the deal with applauding a pilot? It is actually within their job description to take the airplane from the sky to the ground, all part of the gig. If you hadn't yet worked it out, that person sitting in the cockpit with the funky epaulettes is there for no other reason. They have a pilot's licence and stuff – the real deal.

If, in the wake of some terrible mid-flight emergency, Bob from Arbroath, sitting in row F, suddenly volunteers to land the plane and finds himself, against all odds, bringing a loaded 747 to a safe landing then please, clap like the clappers – hug the man and shower him with gifts. If you happen to be on a plane with celebrity canine fluffball Pudsey the Dog and the beast scrambles to action after a mid-air mishap renders the pilot out of action, then clap that little mutt for all it's worth. These would be extraordinary feats. A qualified pilot landing a plane is not a feat. It's specifically what they are there to do. So next time you get the urge to go clap-crazy, just imagine how you would feel if a bunch of random strangers followed you to work and broke into spontaneous applause just because you'd sold a leg of lamb or posted a letter.

And then there's this crock of oddballs...

THE SUNSET

If I hadn't seen this with my own eyes, I could never have believed such a thing.

I was sitting on a hillside in the Tuscan village of Cortona waiting for the sun to go down. All predictable stuff: fifty or so tourists, some cheap red wine and more smartphones than an Apple store. For the Italian holidaymaker, this was the money shot. Who doesn't like a sun, particularly a setting one? Against the verdant terrain of one of the world's most beautiful landscapes, this was going to be a beauty. As the clock ticked towards 8.45 p.m., cameras began to click. The massive red sun was making its way to the other side of the northern hills – *click, click, click*. Just a few seconds to go … it's nearly gone – *click, click, click* – one last chance for the photo of a lifetime – *click*. And with that, the sun finally descended.

There was a brief second of silence. And then something else. *Clap, clap, clap*. It got louder. Lots of clapping. People were actually giving a round of applause … to a sun. Had I missed something? Was this Italian protocol? Was it an ancient Catholic ritual that I had failed to spot in the tour guide? (*Eternal damnation for those whose hands are not sore of clapping post the sun going yonder.*) And what did these people expect to happen? Did they think the sun was about to pop back up and take a bow? Were they mistaken and thought they were actually at some kind of open-air theatre show? Was *I* mistaken and *was* I at an open-air theatre show? No such conspiracy. Just another weird dose of humans being arses. As we left the hillside, I heard one of the tourists say to his wife, 'She was a stunner.' She? *She?* Wow, this old wag hadn't only applauded the sun; he'd assigned a gender to it. Am I living in a different universe?

The next day, it pissed down. I wonder if they clapped for that.

25.

BAD TAT BOZOS

Not many decades ago, if you wanted to see the Tattooed Lady or the Amazing Fat Man, you went to the circus. Now, you just go to Bromley. Standards have dropped.

There are two kinds of people who get tattoos. Those who are philosophically linked to an idea or design and see body art as being as legitimate as any other form of artistry. And those who just fancy the idea of getting a tattoo. It's the second group where all the problems lie.

I've tried to identify whether there was a specific time or vogue that prompted the almost national epidemic of having enormous sections of your body permanently drawn on in the name of fashion. The oxymoronic problem with this (by definition, a fashion *can't* be permanent) should be pretty damn obvious and sound some very loud alarm bells. But apparently not. In the past decade, Brits have taken the art of shit tattoos into another stratosphere. Having badly drawn Indian chiefs, patterns and symbols, icons, messages, stamps and slogans irrevocably etched onto arms, legs, ears, wrists, eyelids and backs is, apparently, a perfectly normal thing to do.

The apocryphal visitor to Planet Earth might just assume

this is merely a craze pursued exclusively by archetypal lash-ridden students after an unhealthy dose of peer pressure. It isn't. Everyone is at it. Even the old folk.

Last summer I spied a women queuing down at the local Costcutter. She was wearing a summer vest, one of those backless numbers that tie up at the top. Unhappily, this allowed the enormity of her grim collection of tats to be displayed to the world. There were more crimes against artwork and taste than I could list here (the curator at the Tate Modern can sleep easy) but what stood out as much as the stamps themselves was that this old dear was a good sixty-five years old. It might have been argued that she'd had all these done years back and is now in a perpetual state of regret (dubious given her clear desire to show them off), but given how rare it would have been back in the '50s to see anyone, let alone a woman, inked up to this level, this was also unlikely.

In this case, there was little doubt: these things were recent. I knew this not because my pigmentation-dar is that good; my eye for fresh ink is not particularly tuned. The reason I was able to swiftly authenticate the age of these markings was because one of them had a date on it. On her neck. It said *Romford 2016*. I don't know what happened in Romford in 2016 (I did look it up and it appears a new Mayor came into office in the May but I'm having severe doubts that the woman decided to mark this occasion with a tat) – but let's be honest, unless she came face to face with God, JFK or Tupac, then what the hell could have been so momentous that she felt an overwhelming desire to permanently brand her own neck with a written celebration? My guess is that whatever it was, her innate desire for the stamp was greater than the event itself; it just felt like the thing to do. After all, tats are cool and a sign of individuality. The fact that two thirds of the population have all decided on the same journey somewhat diminishes the individuality case. Add that to the curious reality that half of these inkings seem more than similar in design, and the case for uniqueness is completely obliterated. But this is where we are. These are not people philosophically attached to an idea or design. They just *want* to have a tattoo. And it almost doesn't matter what it is.

This is not an entirely new phenomenon. Back in the '80s, there was a brief phase when weird people had worthy oriental messages daubed onto their body parts saying odd things like 'Calmness is the Greatest Strength' – a Buddhist-like mantra they clearly felt so strongly about that they had it written in a language that neither they nor anyone they knew could understand (and that's assuming it really *did* say that – it probably just said 'My cat is an arsehole'). Then we had that baffling fad of folk having bits of barbed wire penned onto them, usually around the top of the arm or across the chest. I remember seeing a guy at my local swimming pool who had gone for the barbed look. I'm sure that when this 'dude' was a buffed-up twenty-something, this wiry statement looked pretty reasonable. Back then his chiselled torso was no doubt the perfect platform for the two metres' worth of inked wire that snaked its way from pec to thigh via the toned form of his impressive abs. Fifteen years on, it looked more like something from the Battle of the Somme, the wire now all downtrodden and flimsy as his flabby bits had eradicated this once fine piece of artwork.

And this is really crucial for wannabe tat-wallahs to consider. Having a large amount of body art is part of a package. Your body isn't simply a labelling plate for random designs.

You can't simply decide you want one and then hunt for a pattern to quench that desire; it's all part of a much wider statement. Tattoos look great on David Beckham but ridiculous on Justin Bieber; Amy Winehouse pulled it off but Cher Lloyd looks like an idiot. In the same way that some people suit a hat while others just look like pests, tattoos don't suit everybody or every *body*. If you haven't got the look, swagger or confidence to carry it off then stay away from the parlour.

And just a final thought for one of the more unfathomable penchants in tat-based tomfoolery: the desire to have your kid's birth date written behind your earhole. If you don't know when your kid was born, you probably shouldn't have had one in the first place. But if you genuinely don't remember their birth date due to some sort of amnesiac incident, just buy yourself a nice notebook and write it down. It'll save you money, pain and ridicule, all in one go.

26.

NOEL EDMONDS

Being a kid was a pretty good gig. There's all the obvious stuff: no mortgage, no invoices and no mass panic because you lost three Twitter followers in one week. And then there's all that other lark that stays with you for ever: the three-year-long summer holidays, your first bike, the almost heart-attack-inducing excitement of knowing you're going off to see your cousins in a distant part of the country (usually twenty miles away), that first crush and just about every Christmas. All of these things are indelibly logged into our minds for the rest of time. And then there were Saturday mornings. It was here that I first met Noel Edmonds.

I didn't actually *meet* Noel Edmonds. I just saw him every week on the telly. It just felt like I had met him, like he was my mate. A regular friendly face in my life on a weekly basis. Noel presented Saturday morning TV in the form of *Multi-Coloured Swap Shop* – a marathon-like show of guests, quizzes, features and chaos. Kids' TV had never seen anything quite like this before – this was beyond groundbreaking. You could even call up and speak to Noel himself and have a proper natter with him and his crew (01 811 8055 – for the

Swap Shop generation, that number is engrained into the very core of our brains).

In the world of kids' TV, this was the game changer and pretty much everything that has followed has its roots firmly linked to *MCSS*. As well as frontman Noel, there was also a regular team who joined him each week to add even more verve: Keith Chegwin (Cheggers), Maggie Philbin and the mighty John Craven formed the supporting cast as the nation's kids were taken on a two-and-a-half-hour rollercoaster of complete and unadulterated joy. The comfort and warmth that came from Saturday mornings was like nothing we had experienced before.

When you think of how kids' TV works today, Noel was an interesting choice. He was neither young nor wacky, but nor was he like your dad; he was an entity in his own right. Like a different breed of TV human. I had decided from the off that when I grew up, I wanted to be Noel Edmonds. It was intoxicating; I couldn't think of any better way of earning a living than being Noel – a life of constant, uncompromising fun. It's interesting what time does. Today, I would rather be Douglas Carswell than Noel Edmonds.

It's hard to pinpoint the exact moment that Noel went from hero to weirdo. After *Swap Shop* he still retained an amazing career and made the tricky journey from being the default face of Saturday morning TV to the chosen face of Saturday evenings. He was never off the box. From *The Late, Late Breakfast Show* to *Telly Addicts*, the *Saturday Roadshow* to *House Party*, Noel remained a constant presence and even when the jokes had begun to wear thin and our appetite for gunge and wind-ups began to wane, we didn't really think any the less of Noel. He was a bit dated but he was still our mate – the silky-smooth man off the goggle-box and the most recognisable face in the land. And then he buggered off for about ten years. And came back as a wizard.

Noel had clearly spent his time in the media wilderness overdosing on self-help books and spiritual hokum, because the next time I saw him on the telly he was banging on about something called Cosmic Ordering, a spiritual directive that instructs its followers to write down all of their desires and ambitions onto a piece of paper and three weeks later (four if the spirits are busy) all of those worldly wants will miraculously show up. I've tried it. It doesn't work. If it did, I'd be writing this from a beach in Mauritius with a body like David Beckham, and Boris Johnson as my butler. In short, it's bollocks. Mumbo-jumbo of the highest order. The current state of scientific play shows there is zero evidence that scribbling stuff onto a Post-it note and sticking it on the fridge yields any kind of tangible changes to your life.

Cosmic Ordering sits in the same mad ballpark as the cold-reading con practised by the psychic mob. Basic laws of averages dictate that some events/changes in your life *will* happen regardless. The proponent then highlights this as proof that the gods were working their crafty magic. They spectacularly omit the 99.9 per cent of other things that *didn't* happen. Noel claims that he was given the job as host of *Deal or No Deal* as result of asking the angels to deliver. The angels were clearly a bit confused when the request went in, because the job of fronting the world's most ridiculous game show was actually offered to Chris Evans first.

Noel's journey from showman to shaman had hardly begun.

He had even more spooky tricks up his sleeve. Not only did he tell the world that he is constantly followed around by two giant glowing orbs (maybe Cheggers monkeying around?) but he also claims to see auras in the sky, describing them as 'giant writhing silver sperms'. The man is crackers.

More recently, he found himself in the receiving end of a public hiding after telling a cancer sufferer on Twitter that it was entirely possible that his disease was caused by having a *bad attitude*, adding that it was a scientific fact that bad energy can cause fatal diseases. The man politely replied by telling Noel to stick to beard trimming.

But Noel wasn't done. As our spiritual oncologist continued getting berated on social media, the mainstream boys chipped in. Phil and Holly wanted a word. This must have been a tough call for Schofield, who I'm pretty sure would previously have held Edmonds in the same reverential esteem as I had. Nonetheless, and ever the pro, Phil drilled down to the nitty-gritty of Edmonds's insane claims. Turns out Noel puts such cancer-curing assistance down to an electronic yoga pad that fires positive vibes up ya fundamentals and rebalances your bits and pieces. Ergo negative things like cancer can be tackled and eradicated. He said that he had utilised this very kit to cure himself of disease and even uses it on his dog. He seemed incredulous that we weren't all on the same page. The ITV duo were not convinced and neither was the public. Noel disappeared with his tail between his legs, and the manufacturers of the very device he talks of completely disassociated themselves from any such claim.

Noel's dalliances with the world of positive energy continues. He recently added magic filters to his water taps in order to produce positive water, presumably with the aim of maintaining his karma and keeping that new-found career trajectory going in a positive direction. Three weeks later, *Deal or No Deal* was cancelled. After years of screwing over viewers with a non-game game show, Channel 4 finally pulled the plug. Maybe that Cosmic Ordering thing does work after all.

I'm not sure there's any way back for Noel. In the credibility stakes, he's damaged goods. You can't mooch around the place claiming to solve cancer and telling people that all their worldly dreams are just a to-do list away without folk thinking you're bat-shit crazy. It's a big fat shame. Saturday mornings have never quite been the same. If any lazy commissioner is thinking of bringing back a kind of *Swap Shop* reboot thing (let's face it, someone somewhere is probably planning exactly this) then please think again. The idea of Noel floating above that desk while plugged into his pulse mat dispensing spiritual wisdom to confused children is too much. That said, if you add in Cheggers in a kind of Ron Weasley capacity and Craven as Gandalf with that massive stick to beat Noel around the head when he starts going all supernatural on us, then maybe I'll pencil in those Saturday mornings again. Until then, I'll stick with pseudo celebs cooking beef Wellington in a pretend kitchen in west London.

27.

PLASTIC PROTESTERS

I guess you have to blame the internet. Sir Tim Berners-Lee has a lot to answer for.

In 2003, the UK saw the biggest ever protest of its kind. Almost a million people took to the streets to rally against Blair's war in Iraq. The Stop the War Coalition had mounted an incredible campaign against what they saw as an illegal invasion. Their message was clear and they wanted fellow Brits to join them as they marched through the streets of London. Old ladies and small children alike gathered in the capital for the mother of all protests. Banners were made, coaches were booked and leaflets handed out across the UK. On the morning of 15 February, the peaceful march began. Three and a half miles of people (just let that sink in) walked peacefully through the capital to tell the UK government that they needed to rethink their foreign policy and call off their action in the Middle East.

What marks out this event more than anything else is that the entire thing was arranged before social media existed. There was no Facebook or Twitter, no super-fast broadband and websites still looked as if they had been knocked up using crayons. Looking back, it's almost impossible to imagine that such an occasion could have been organised without the aid of the online components that today we take for granted. Regardless of whether you agree with the sentiment of the protest, you can't fail to be in awe of how the whole damn thing was put together.

Today it's a very different picture. Protests and rallies are organised at the touch of a button. If you weren't happy with the EU referendum result then a march can be organised within forty-eight hours. If you think that Jeremy Corbyn needs some TLC, just cut and paste a few Facebook posts and a hundred people will dutifully show up. It doesn't even have to be an issue that is happening in this country: you can get angry with Israel, be outraged by the Louisiana Police Department or sympathise with the Buddhist monks of Tibet and still marshal a healthy presence, all waving wonky placards in support of their desired causes.

Protesting, as they say, has become a *thing*. You don't have to be philosophically attached to the issue or even know very much about it. If you're willing to show up then you are clearly one of the good guys. One of the ones who *care*. A swift message on your Twitter timeline will give you the details (*the government are evil and we need to wave some signs to prove this*) and all you have to do is jump on a train.

Shortly after the UK voted to leave the EU, the good and the great decided that they didn't much like the democratic decision of the British people so they were going to have a large protest and make some noise. What better way to prove that you're a nice person than to have serval dozen photos on your Facebook page of you attending a Westminster rally while waving a blue flag that three days before you couldn't have picked out of a flag ID parade if it had a massive red arrow pointing towards it.

As folk were gathering on College Green to display their virtue to the world, I was on a train coming into work. It was slightly busier than usual. I was among the protesters. About half a dozen of them were on their way into town and I had found myself sharing the same carriage. But these were not the pro-EU people. These were the Corbyn people. This was an entirely separate protest that had been hastily put together to tell hard-working socialists that they weren't socialist enough if they didn't support Jeremy. In fact, they were the scum of the earth – secret Tories, the lot of 'em. Anyone who didn't support Jezza was a filthy blue: the substance of their argument was that simple. One of them was wearing a T-shirt that proclaimed in big red letters 'Tom Watson is a class traitor', another carried some leaflets that showed a picture of Tony Blair over the slogan 'Hurry Up and Die', and a third man was drinking Special Brew like it was his last ever drink. This was central casting with bells on. Not to stereotype, but if you wanted to write a booklet on how Jeremy Corbyn can *definitely* lose the next election, these three would be on the front cover.

I never did work out whether this particular day had been earmarked as National Protest About Anything You Like Day, but as I approached Leicester Square to go into LBC, I could hear their distant din of a chant. I couldn't make out the specific words but it was that unmistakable sound of a protesting collective. Were these the Corbyn mob? Were they the pro-EU massive? Neither. These were the Black Lives Matter brigade.

Only a halfwit would suggest that we have achieved full-on racial harmony in the UK. But I'm pretty darn sure that we don't have anything like the problems the United States have when it comes to the police/race issue. This point was clearly lost on the fifty or so people that were about to march by. This lot were not merely attempting to show a kinship with their American cousins but seemed to be arguing that the UK has an identical issue. The crowd was young, average age maybe twenty, and many were carrying badly photocopied images of young American criminals who had met their end at the hands of the Feds. Did they even know who these people were? Most seemed keener on taking grinning selfies as they made their way through crowds of confused tourists and head-scratching locals. Why the hell was a protest against the Baton Rouge Police Department happening in Leicester Square? But of course it wasn't *really* a protest: it was a day out. Rosa Parks would have been spinning in her sacred grave.

Social media had clearly played a blinder here, and at least three marches/rallies had all happened in one day. All no doubt organised within twenty-four hours. We can't turn back the clock but we can watch and weep at how protesting has lost its verve. The Stop the War march was an event. The sweat and tears that were put in to organise such a massive display of public opinion fuels the entire power of the message. Clicking on a Facebook page may well be the contemporary way of displaying outrage but it will never carry the same impressive levels of authenticity of what went before it.

This is now an uncomfortable dichotomy for rally-mongers. The internet, which should be seen as the bastion of free speech and the very tool that has allowed the quiet voice a safe space, has become a victim of its own success. As protests become as regular a sight as buses, those all-important messages and campaigns aren't simply diluted but virtually obliterated.

28.

CITY CYCLISTS

In 2011, East Riding Council in Yorkshire banned kite-flying on their beaches in case someone gets hurt by a polythene owl falling out of the sky. A fine of £500 could be imposed if you are caught breaching the rule. In the same year, Butlin's banned bumping in bumper cars. Anyone caught carrying out an act of bumping in a bumper car would be banned from ever bumping again. Over in Tyne and Wear, they were getting all funny about sack races on school sports days and decided the best way to avoid a kid grazing their arm was to ban the event completely: sack races were made illegal. Down in Bromley, they decreed that bin men should avoid bending over too far into bins, just in case a troublesome bin bag gave them a bit of gyp in the back department. And the British Legion banned the practice of giving out pins with poppies, just in case someone stabs themselves in the lapel while trying to attach one.

My man down at the Health and Safety Department tells me that there is no other country in the world that is quite so governed by petty rules and utterly bonkers regulations. When it comes to bureaucratic mumbo-jumbo, the UK takes the gold at every level.

We can all comprehend a sensible bit of guidance. We understand, for example, why it should be illegal to leave a recently sharpened scythe in a child's ball pool and we totally get why banisters in old people's homes are not allowed to be made out of plasticine. But we have now found ourselves in a fuzzy, upside-down world where daft authoritarian edicts replace and usurp the basic laws of common sense.

But there is one massive and unfathomable exception.

Despite the batty roll-call of statist guff that emanates from local and central government under the auspices of making us all nice and safe, it is still perfectly legal to ride a knackered old bike in the same piece of road space as a 34-ton truck. Not only is it legal, it is actively encouraged. There's not even a law that suggests a helmet might be a wise move.

In the past decade, the UK has gone nuts for the bike. Local authorities, ministers and fitness gurus have all jumped on the bicycle bandwagon with the triple aim of decongesting our streets, saving the environment and increasing personal health. What's not to like?

London is probably the best example of a city tripping over itself to prove its *two wheels good, four wheels bad* credentials. They were the first out of the traps with a city-wide cycle hire scheme and have since spent hundreds of millions of pounds of taxpayers' money digging up already desperately needed road space to accommodate a pastime taken up by 1 per cent of the population.

Every borough wanted a taste of cycling supremacy and if that meant several years' worth of disruption, then so be it: roads were narrowed, pavements widened and cycle lanes installed. When the work was complete and big chiefs from the council had satisfied themselves of their worthy contributions to modern life, they narrowed a few more roads and planted another batch of cycle lanes. If you haven't seen it, it's hard to explain just how evangelical these obsessives have become. Notionally, it's a hard one to argue – less traffic and more bikes is surely a progressive cocktail. The reality is somewhat different.

I recently clocked a lunatic on a Boris Bike riding on a stretch of road called the Embankment. He'd decided that the optimum way to cycle on one of the busiest and most danger-ous pieces of city road was to go no-handed while reading a book. Once in a while he glanced around at the surrounding city, taking in the sights. He eventually reattached his hands to the supplied handlebars but this was only a temporary blip while he negotiated the best way to jump the red light. A few honks and curses later, he's back gliding down the road, utterly oblivious to his growing CV of idiocy. The book-reading thing, surprisingly, isn't totally rare – it sits alongside texting, phon-ing and rolling cigs – you see it lots. The red-light-jumping farce is far more common than cyclists like to confess and I'm still a tad bemused by just how little is made of this. But none of these things were his greatest offence. What had put this moron into a new stratosphere of insanity was that he was riding his bike on a major road while just two feet away from him was 900 million quids' worth of super-safe, segregated cycling highway. This bozo had deliberately opted *not* to use the very thing that was built to accommodate his every need. In fairness to him, no one else was using the cycle highway either. It's a rare day to see it anywhere near busy.

The kamikaze loon with the book may well be exceptional

in his blatancy, but he's certainly not a rarity when it comes to the broader of issue of mixing cars and trucks with cycles. Despite the many miles of cycling highways that now snake their way through the capital city, most of the place is still – and always will be – cycle lane-free. The Victorian infrastructure of the place was always going to dictate limitations on bike lanes. This leaves the average cyclist, whose desired route doesn't coincide with where the shiny new cycle paths have been placed, little or no choice but to use the conventional road space.

The upshot of this is that tens of thousands of two-wheel travellers are irreversibly paired with their motorised counterparts on some of the country's most congested roads. The risk-taking is off the scale as cyclists place themselves alongside, in front of and in between several hundred thousand tons' worth of trucks and cars every day. Whether this is born out of arrogant oblivion, or possibly the immunity they mistakenly feel the constant pro-cycling argument has bought them, is hard to tell. The grim statistics of death and injury speak for themselves yet the fundamentalists down at City Hall plough on regardless with their worthy experiment.

You don't have to be a health and safety expert to know that riding a Raleigh Chopper through Piccadilly Circus at rush hour is probably not a good idea. Yet it's this very scenario that will earn you applause from the Mayor and politicians alike. Just don't drop any litter as you go – the authorities take a dim view of such blatant levels of irresponsibility.

29.

NJSS (NON-JUDGEMENTAL SPOUSE SYNDROME)

There's a couple walking in front of me. They are clearly in love. She has her arm around his waist and his is comfortably wrapped over her shoulder. It's a lovely sunny day and, in an often ugly world, a lovely sight. What could be nicer than two little lovebirds on the mooch?

But then something happens. All is not good. The man begins to make a terrible noise. A kind of guttural sound. It gets louder. I notice his shoulders begin to gyrate – he appears to be trying to catch his breath. The sound has now gone full volume. His head is motioning forwards and backwards. Should I call for emergency help? Whatever is going on, this isn't good.

But there is something even more peculiar. Something out of place. The couple are still walking arm in arm. There appears to be no reference to this man's clear predicament. This is all very odd. The guttural noise becomes nasal. And then he stops. And that's when it happens. In the middle of Bromley High Street, Casanova coughs up and projectile-spits out a massive lump of snot. I'm even uncomfortable writing the damn words. This was beyond grim, even by Bromley standards. Thank God no one was in the firing range because this thing leapt out of his kisser with the speed of an Andy Murray serve, landing just below the window frame of Superdrug. He gave a little cough and he and his good lady continued on their romantic walk. There was no comment from either of them.

Charing Cross Station, London. I'm in the ticket hall. The man behind the counter has my attention for all the wrong reasons. I'm not hearing his advice about return journeys to Ramsgate. I'm mesmerised by something else. Ticket Boy is clearly a fan of the Wrigley's. It's a disturbing sight. I've experienced overambitious gum chewers before and it's not that unusual to see these filthy swine chomping away like they're eating a fence post, but this character had a PhD in it.

Seeing a human jaw open and close that widely and rapidly for the sole purpose of chewing a tiny piece of gum is a disturbing sight. It's like his gob is on autopilot. Up and down it goes, clacking away at a good 50mph. His jaw couldn't get any lower if you surgically detached it and glued it to his kneecap. And then there's the sound. Like the noise of a hand dipping in and out of a gooey peat bog. Is this a facial tick? A kind of psychological thing? Or is he just a monumental filth-bag who wouldn't know good manners if they shot up his trouser leg? The smart money is on the latter.

The chewing becomes even louder and more urgent as he attempts to spit out his words. Why aren't his colleagues saying anything? He's got a room full of people around him – wouldn't one of them pitch up and tell him to get a grip? But I've noticed something else. Something even more disturbing. He's wearing a wedding ring. Someone, somewhere, decided that this is the man they wanted to spend the rest of their life with.

And it's that last point that puts him, and others like him, into the 67. This isn't actually about noisy eaters, gum chewers or weirdos who think that coughing out a greenie in Bromley High Street is acceptable. That would be too obvious – it's a given that these people are surplus to the human gene pool. This is about their other halves. Their wives, husbands or partners. It's that lot that that need dragging under the spotlight for a swift naming and shaming.

If you were out on a first date and noticed, while you were tucking into a tasty pepperoni, that your new-found love was clearly incapable of eating a meal without sounding like a warthog, wouldn't that be the end of the date? Isn't that a deal breaker? Regardless of how gorgeous and humorous you thought they were, this would surely be the point when you realised that this was going no further. There could be no second date. Quite aside from the impossibility of taking the animal anywhere for fear of ridicule from friends and fellow diners, do you really want to snog the face of someone who eats food like a Neanderthal?

Evidently, some don't care. Who are *these* people? Who could sit at home on a cosy Saturday evening watching *The X Factor* while your partner polished off a pack of Hubba Bubba like he was chewing on a Jack Russell? Who is the person who snuggles up to Spit Boy to go jiggy-bound, knowing full well what has been in his mouth just hours before? How can that not matter?

We've already more than established on this journey that humans do very strange things. The propensity to deviate from that unwritten template of acceptability is more than evident. But most of these blatant and unfathomable acts only happen because there's no one around to stop the perpetrator and educate their wonky brains. If you happen to be dating anyone who sits in the above sector, do the nation a favour and next time they go off-piste in the 'This is totally unacceptable' department, kick them in the throat and leave. Failure to do so renders you just as much of an unacceptable arse as them.

And if you should find yourself in south London and you hear a man making noises that appear to signal almost certain death, forget puckering up for a bit of mouth-to-mouth resuscitation, just leg it: it's probably that same dirty scuzz merchant gearing up for another swift session of gob-mania.

30.

INANE AND BOASTFUL TWITTER MONKEYS

Anyone who tweets the single word 'Morning' on their Twitter feed should be dragged from their homes, tarred and feathered and left in the sun for a month. It's just bloody annoying. Morning, my arse.

When you speak to die-hard tech monkeys who were there at the very inception of the internet, they will regale you with tales of the first news sites and the original chat rooms. It wasn't always pretty: these first online debating arenas were serious business for serious people and dog eat dog was the order of the day – a kind of intergalactic Wild West. There was no precedent for these guys. No one had ever seen human interaction in this way before; it was new, exciting and, for the most part, brutal. Literally a game changer in our journey.

Things move on. In the same way that hardcore punk fans almost lost the will to live when Captain Sensible of The Damned decided to record the foot-tapping melodic shite-fest 'Happy Talk', these original online warriors can't quite believe that the sacred soil that is the internet is now being used for knuckleheads to write things like 'Morning'. It was never meant to be this way.

But you can't stop progress or coerce evolution. We are where we are and have little choice but to accept new realities. The online world may well, for the most part, be our best friend, but, simultaneously, it also becomes the embarrassing uncle. Social media does indeed bring us a plethora of lay philosophers and brilliant minds but, conversely, it's also become the playground for the chronically un-self-aware.

Writing 'Morning' might, on the face of it, seem innocuous. But it isn't. It's full of self-importance and pleads for endorsement. What is meant to be the response to this? Are you supposed to just say 'Morning' back? Does this mean others will come on board and say 'Morning' to you too? Will your followers then kick in with more mornings? Does the original morning-monger then say 'Morning' again? How many mornings can you have in one morning, for God's sake? It's like the opening scene of Python's *The Meaning of Life*. Morning.

Inanity and social media are natural bedfellows but that doesn't mean we shouldn't ponder and expose them for the utter clowns they are. They come in many forms and the Location Boasters are up there with the best of them. I spotted some Herbert tweeting this one recently. It was accompanied by a photo of a sun-kissed view of St Tropez: 'My office for the next few days'.

Oh, do belt up. Do you have any idea what an utter cretin you sound? Yes, it's bully for you that your very important job in PR takes you to some nice places, but why the desperate need to brag about it to the rest of us? Maybe I should get my Auntie Pam to tweet some shelves of biscuits in Tesco with the same caption. The only possible point of a tweet like this is to tell all of your followers how much better your life is than theirs. Get a grip.

I recently clocked that girl Lisa Snowdon doing exactly the same thing. She posted a glaring snap of herself reclining on a huge million-pound yacht in a swimsuit. She wrote: 'Sun on my skin and wind in my hair.'

Good for you, Lisa, and well done on the poetic nature of your wording, but what exactly is your point in tweeting that? Why the need to tell the world? I'm sure Carol in Barnsley doing the late turn at the Tickled Trout felt a million dollars when that popped into her Twitter feed.

They can't help themselves. Telling people how great their life is has become the order of the day. The supercilious guff that spews from brain to keyboard is as automatic to them as getting out of bed. Here's another unfathomable: 'Have I missed anything?' (written without irony).

Where do you want me to start? Well, since you last posted, the Prime Minister has resigned, there's been an attempted coup in the Middle East, President Trump has made some noises about climate change and I won twenty-five quid on a scratch card.

Was that the answer you were looking for? I suspect not. In fact, even you didn't know the answer you were looking for. You just wanted *an* answer. A reply to your utterly meaningless question. I suspect that if I did tweet back with a crib sheet of world events, there would be no reply. The tweet was never designed to engage in meaningful conversation, it was merely an attempt to reaffirm the importance of their own existence by counting how many people actually cared enough to respond.

I just took a cursory sweep of Twitter. There's an entire army of them out there: *just got up, big day ahead, life isn't fair, justice, tired, whoops...* What do they want?

Against my better judgement, I recently got into a minor row on this very point. One of these loons had written the word 'Joy' on his feed. Nothing else, just 'Joy'. I stepped in and asked what the actual reason was for the post, what it meant. He was fast to reply. Piss off, he wrote. Wow, two words, we're getting there. My comment had clearly rattled him because he then sent off a barrage of tweets explaining to me that it was his feed and he could write what the hell he likes. His contention was simple:

> @IanCollinsUK I wouldn't come around your house and tell you where to place your armchairs and sofa because that would be none of my business. My tweets are none of your business. #PissOff

This is balls. What I do in my own front room is indeed my business but if I posted a photo on a public forum of my purple three-seater, it then becomes everybody else's. There would be reaction and comment. That's because it's Twitter – a public forum. People post things with the specific intention of being noticed. Ergo, other people reply and judge.

We need to fight fire with fire. I'm thinking we go for an international response campaign to stave off the weird, vain and boastful. If this lot are really that enamoured of one-word meaningless tweets then let's meet them at the gates. I never thought I would write this sentence, because it tends to drive me round the pipe when other people do, but on this occasion, there's no other way: let's get a hashtag going. I'm pretty sure that if we all replied #Tosser every time one of these inane clowns reared their heads, it's just possible they would go away.

Try to imagine Smug-Face McDougall waking up and sending off their daft *Morning* tweet only to have thirty-seven people call them a tosser for their troubles. It's a beautiful thought. My guess is that they won't do it again. Job done.

31.

VIRTUE SIGNALLERS

This is how it was first explained to me:

Virtue signalling is the popular modern habit of indicating that one has virtue merely by expressing disgust or favour for certain political ideas or cultural happenings.

And we all know one of two of these characters...

'But global warming will kill us all in twenty years. We must act.'

'Which aspect of global warming bothers you most?'

'Er... all of it.'

Brilliant.

Aligning yourself with important ideas or political issues without knowing jack shit about them isn't new. The human condition throws up all manner of unfathomable quirks, and the desire to be seen as a nice person is certainly one of them. When my mate Chaz first uttered his new-found concern over the future of the planet, I was taken aback not by the issue itself (although he had never once mentioned this before) but by his desire to get very angry about something that he seriously knew nothing about. It took about two questions to expose the game. He wanted – and needed – to be seen as someone on the *kind* side of the argument. He thought that uttering plat-itudes about corporate greed and rainforests marked him out as one of the good guys. His concern wasn't for Amazonian river parrots or the oil-filled seas of the Western Pacific, it was to be seen as someone who *cares*.

Virtue signalling applies to all sides of the political divide, from the pseudo Marxist whose knowledge on the theory of surplus value amounts to the square root of sod all to the gobby capitalist who wouldn't know Adam Smith if he jumped into his bed with a name badge on. All sides are guilty of playing a game where the aim is not merely to proffer another side to an argument or debate but to illustrate and signal that their view is the *morally* superior one. Once you've convinced yourself of that, you're pretty much free to malign, castigate and libel your opposition as much as you like. After all, you now have God on your side.

But there is also a Premier League version of virtue signal-ling that takes the desire to occupy that moral high ground to totally new levels. This is where you simply make up an argument or view, and then argue against it with the sole pur-pose of being seen as a much more decent and rational person than your invented enemy. The straw man technique. Nowhere was this game more pervasive than post the EU referendum of 2016.

It was all going so well. Brits were about to be given a choice between leaving or remaining in the EU. It was a crack-ing few weeks of campaigning and pretty much every night we were treated to a TV bonanza of debates and lively dis-cussion as each side laid out their respective stalls. Cameron explained how we needed to remain in order to protect future generations from a life of isolationism; Boris bumbled his way to an Independence Day-style frenzy; a woman called Andrea whom we had never heard of before told us that it was vital to the future of human life that we left; Chancellor George explained that the cost of bread would rise to £18 a loaf if we didn't remain; and Nigel warned us that some foreign folk might arrive at your house and try to bum your dog if we didn't get the hell out. All in all, a good cross-section of views. Both sides played the mischief card, but so long as you used your own brain (and did some of your own research) we were broadly treated to an even debate.

On 23 June, Brits dutifully made our way to the ballot box to cast our votes. Twenty-four hours later, we were out of the EU. Technically. Within days, a right hullabaloo had broken out. The Remainers were not happy. They made the extraordinary claim that the vote was not authentic because it was too close (48 per cent to 52 per cent). They also added that the arguments for leaving had been so venal as to essentially declare the result null and void. This was heady stuff. We're used to seeing the EU themselves try to sneak in second referendums when things don't quite go their way but this was the *people* – albeit on the losing side – who had decreed that the only way to make things fair would be to hold a *second* vote.

A week later, the protests began. Seeing was believing. A debate that had started with the straightforward question 'Should the UK remain a member of the EU or leave?' had somehow morphed into a more curious question: 'Are you a nice person or a mad racist?' How in the name of Jean-Claude Junker did we get here? But it was this level of crass polarity that formed the post-referendum narrative.

Naturally, social media would be the place to mobilise the masses. Meanwhile, the good and the great from the world of journalistic commentariat would inform the debate with lengthy columns and TV appearances about why those who voted Leave were essentially a bunch of nasty gits who hated foreigners. It's difficult to think of any other area of life where you would be allowed to casually denounce and revile 17 million people. But let's not get bogged down with the details: the scene was now set for the greatest display of virtue signalling in modern history.

There were dozens of reasons to make a decision to vote Leave. From sovereignty to TTIP (Transatlantic Trade and Investment Partnership – which should frighten the life out of the most ardent of Europhiles), low wage scales to the sheer non-democratic nature of the entire construct. But it was immigration – and only immigration – that the signallers had selected as their weapon of choice. In the wake of a small number of pretty unsavoury attacks on migrants and property (attacks that one has to reasonably assume would have still happened had we voted to Remain) the Euro-enthusiasts had decreed that this was what defined a Leaver. There was now a clear battle between two sides: nice and not nice.

A little over a week after the referendum, tens of thousands marched upon the UK's capital to make some noise. In order to showcase their credentials as decent people, they had made placards and banners that said things like 'If you voted leave you are a racist c***', 'Old white people should die', 'I'm not a shit Brit, I'm a proud European', and 'F*** off Brexiters'. The irony was almost too much, but in the best traditions of virtue signalling that really doesn't matter – remember, you have absolute good on your side, so calling your enemy as many expletives as your lexicon can muster is no different to libelling Chairman Mao or Stalin, and nobody would blame you for doing that.

In spite of the fact that this was supposed to be a demo about the future of a political and economic trading bloc, the badges and mantras were desperately trying to tell a different story: 'Not in my name', 'We love you, EU', 'People Unite'. Leaping lizards! This had now turned into a full-blown John and Yoko-style love-in. This was more Woodstock than Westminster and those involved were tripping over themselves to prove their worth as decent humans. To compound their position as Euro-friendly people, they had developed a dual campaign of wearing a little safety pin in order to cement their niceness even further and to show fellow Europeans that they loved them lots. What the hell is that about? You don't need to self-identify as a *non*-racist, any more than you need to wear a badge to show that you aren't a serial killer or a house breaker; the default human position is that we aren't any of these things in the first place.

As I watched events unfold on the TV news, I wondered how many of this mob really knew anything about the EU. Could they name a single European Commissioner? Did they know who Schuman or Monnet were? Could they talk about the wider significance of the 1951 Franco-German coal agreement? One young girl who had an EU flag painted on her face (with two of the stars missing – tut) was asked why she loved the EU. She replied, 'The NHS' – amazing. This campaign had little to do with the real issues about the European Union and everything to do with signalling virtue.

It was also more than a little disturbing to see the elderly (who had voted in larger numbers to leave) being cruelly singled out and ripped apart for their views. This was the one group who had known a world *pre*-EU (and had lived through and fought in wars), had experienced life during the entire EU experiment and had now concluded that it hadn't worked out. Arguably the *most* qualified group to comment and opine on the issue. Their views were now being trounced by the likes of flag-face girl and her daft crew.

Similarly, proud working-class people whose sense of disenfranchisement had only grown under the EU flag were being berated. I've lost count of how many debates I have seen (and hosted) about why this demographic were not getting more involved in the political process – why they didn't engage more? Well, this time they did get stuck in and voted in large numbers. They were now paying a price for exercising that democratic right with casual accusations of being vile subhuman xenophobes who couldn't possibly have known what they were really voting for.

Casting a vote for Leave wasn't mad, outrageous or strange. Intellectually, it was a perfectly logical move. The EU is *not* a democratic institution. You might favour its existence and believe that on balance it sort of works, but its inception and subsequent growth have blown away all conventional rules of democracy in a way that would make Kim Jong-un sit up and blush. At its heart, the EU is a corporate trading block – an institution designed, above all other considerations, to further and enhance the portfolios and profit margins of privately owned conglomerates and billionaire business bods. There's a good reason why just about every moneyed type on the planet is vehemently pro its existence. Those who speak with such nauseous and unquestioning thirst for constructs such as TTIP are really in no position to be playing any moral cards.

As I continued to watch the TV news, College Green had now become a full-on anti-racist rally, with the worthy masses arguing against their invented enemy. I wondered how many of this lot would also have shown up to an anti-capitalist rally or to protest against the chronic injustice of globalisation and things like TTIP. I'm pretty damn sure that about 90 per cent of them would show up to those demos too. Such blatant contradiction didn't matter right now: today's selected narrative was about love and kindness and, for the moment, this suited their angst just fine.

So here's the thing. I voted Remain. I'm not proud of the lack of passion I employed to arrive at that decision but it was probably similar to many others who voted the same way. The EU project has been rolling along for over forty years and to dismantle and unpack four decades' worth of legislation and policy is nothing short of a massive ball-ache; a gamble I wasn't prepared to take. Those who voted differently, however, should be defended for their basic right to do so.

There were myriad reasons as to why over 17 million people wanted to get the hell off the Brussels gravy train. There's nothing shameful or controversial in seeing the country's future in a different way. For the self-obsessed bully boys who need to characterise Leavers as fanatical, right-wing, foreign-hating nut-jobs with images of Eugène Terre'Blanche tattooed on their arses, your thinking is not only illogical, unpleasant and dumb but flies straight in the face of the very democratic process that virtue signallers constantly claim to support.

32.

JAMIE OLIVER

When Jamie Oliver first pitched up on TV in the '90s with a show called *The Naked Chef*, I was hooked. The programme was set in Jamie's own bachelor-pad kitchen: an impressive affair with huge saucepans, trendy wooden blinds and more shiny gadgets than Currys. Who was this gobby funster who had invaded my screen? I watched with awe and envy as he went about his day cooking stuff in the coolest way a man can cook. He cut up ingredients with his hands, smacked up chunks of meat with his fists and weighed stuff with his palms. If he ran out of food, he simply slid down his banister onto his equally cool moped to fetch more supplies. If his dishes needed that extra zing, he had a boxed herb garden hanging out of his kitchen window – impressive. I had no idea how he financed this curious lifestyle; all I knew was that our new chef on the block was a game changer in the crowded world of televised cookery.

To add to the picture, he didn't talk like most people do on TV. He spluttered his words to camera in a way that compounded his carefree attitude to food and life. He seemed unbothered about image and style; he was all about the cooking.

And when he'd completed his simple but mouth-watering dishes, a bunch of trendy mates would show up for a dinner party. Life looked pretty tasty in the world of Jamie Oliver.

But then I discovered something that utterly shocked me. Something I hadn't factored in. I simply hadn't seen it. Others have since told me that they knew from the outset. I had been too busy admiring his Le Creuset collection to pay enough attention. It turns out that despite that cheeky Essex exterior and casual bluster, Jamie Oliver is, all things considered, a bit of a bell-end. Even writing this, I'm still shocked by this revelation. How did I not notice?

His climb from singleton to international businessman has been impressive: from lucrative TV deals to a library's worth of cook books and series of restaurants and eateries to rival any chef on the planet. Jamie Oliver is big business. But it all went horribly wrong when he decided that he wasn't wholly satisfied with merely being a chef. He wanted to be a Messiah too. Jamie had decreed that knocking out pies and pasta for a living no longer fulfilled his true calling in life. He wanted to educate the world into the evils of sugar and the perils of unhealthy diets. He wanted our little ones better fed and was determined to realign the planet's relationship with food and health. Jamie was to become the Bob Geldof of munch.

It all began with his high-profile campaign to get kids to stop eating chips. An admirable project, but perhaps only slightly less ambitious than trying to get the Inuit people to stop using snow. Jamie travelled the country imparting his wisdom to teachers, politicians and kids alike. He broke bread with the PM and even enlisted the British Army. From Kidbrooke to County Durham, Jamie's one-man crusade to save our nation's kids from the perils of Turkey Twizzlers was under way. There was talk of schools removing junk from school menus, and ministers rallied to associate themselves with the worthy cause. A dinner lady called Nora was also drafted in to guide Jamie through the tricky area of telling kids that a bowl of broccoli is far better for you than a bucket of Haribo. And to make sure the message reached its maximum audience, the whole thing was filmed by a TV company. By a happy coincidence, Jamie also owned the TV company, so that was handy.

We all watched week after week as Jamie and Nora tried their darndest to rewire chubby kids into the joys of healthy eating. In the best traditions of reality TV, there were tears, there were rows and there were plenty of cliffhanging moments to seduce us into watching the next episode. At one point the drama really intensified as Nora and Jamie almost came to blows, with the dinner lady informing the chef: 'Basically, for your business model to work, it's essential to sell crap.' This was not a happy ship. But Jamie wasn't giving up. Eventually things were smoothed over and Nora – by this stage suffering from culinary Stockholm syndrome – was back on side. The duo set to work closing tuck shops, limiting the fried stuff and trying to tell lazy parents that their kids' health wasn't solely the responsibility of the school.

And it was that last point where the holes began to appear. Whatever worthy intentions Oliver & Co. might have had, they were on a hiding to nothing. If dieticians and even morticians had been unable to educate stupid parents into the dangers of filling your kid's heart valves with fat and sugar then the chances were a TV chef wasn't about to do it either.

The school dinners campaign descended into chaos.

Promised budgets weren't delivered, ministers went a bit quiet, school tuck shops were reopened and kids didn't stop liking chips. At one point a couple of enterprising parents, who clearly disagreed with their children eating a healthier diet, took up their own initiative and started flogging burgers to fat-starved kids through the school fence, resulting in Jamie branding one of them a 'big old scrubber'. But name-calling didn't seem to bother them. 'I just don't like Jamie and what he stands for,' said one. 'He's forcing our kids to become more picky about their food.' Er, yes, that *is* kind of the point. Idiot.

The school dinner initiative crumbled mainly because you can't recalibrate children's health solely via a reality TV show. It also failed because honing in on what kids eat at school is only a tiny part of the problem. If it ain't happening at home then the whole thing comes tumbling down. On top of that, Jamie Oliver is not Kofi Annan. But all was not lost. The value of Jamie's own group of companies sky-rocketed during the airing of the programme and bookings for his restaurants went through the roof. Every cloud. Time to launch another campaign.

This time, Jamie was going for gold. It wasn't just kids he had in his sights, but the entire nation. Jamie Oliver was about to wean us all off the wicked and toxic substance that is sugar. And this time the government were onside. After lengthy battles that saw our Jamie make the very reasonable point that lobbing seven spoonfuls of sugar into a single can of cola can't be good for our collective health (and the eventual bill to the NHS) George Osborne, the then Chancellor, decreed that a sugar tax would come into place. It would not only be good for the future health of our little ones, but raise £500 million in the process.

It's hard to know where to start with the numerous flaws in all of this. Firstly, there was to be no ban on sugar itself. It would merely be more expensive when purchased within a drink – just 6p on a litre of fizz. You don't have to be a financial futurist to figure out that cola-guzzling die-hards aren't about to stop over a matter of 6p. The idea fails right there. The other gaping hole here is that you can walk into any fried chicken shop (most towns boast about 500 of them), buy forty-eight pieces of Southern-fried chook and a coke but only the latter will be subject to the new government levy. Whatever sugary compounds lurk within the chicken will be ignored. But these things were not the most farcical aspect of Jamie's healthy eating campaign.

Last summer I went to a place called Bicester Village, one of those large outdoor shopping outlets selling cheap designer clobber. In the middle of the village was an impressive-looking hot dog van. But this wasn't just any old hot dog van. This was *Jamie's* hot dog van. It's called Jamie Oliver's Fabulous Feasts and they knock out all sorts of delicious fast food to hungry shoppers. I assume this is directly owned by our TV chef or franchised out for a small fortune. Either way, it's his name on the tin and that's clearly the attraction. I ordered one of the hot dogs. Man alive.

The dog could, quite literally, have been a dog – it was massive. A foot's worth of sausage, beautifully fried, sprinkled with onions and covered with lashings of tomato sauce and mustard. This was the Premier League of hot dogs. Seven quids' worth (not a typo) of utter joy. But there could be little doubt (without the need to take it down to a laboratory) that this thing was filled with enough unhealthy fodder to down a small army. Delicious it was; healthy it most certainly wasn't. The Ministry of Defence should go into partnership with Jamie on this. Forget driving tanks over the hills of the Middle East – just drop a couple of Oliver's burger trucks into the desert and leave them there. After thirty minutes your enemy will either be so stuffed they'll lose the will to fight or they will have died through sugar poisoning.

I've lost count of how many times Jamie has pitched up on TV to shout and rant about the dangers of the white stuff. Yet here he is flogging the very things that cause the problem. A swift look into his business empire will show you not only a plethora of sugar-filled recipes in his cook books but that his numerous restaurants and outlets are all serving fattening, sugary, calorific grub on a daily basis. Is there not a clash here? The Oliver Empire claims to be doing their bit by offering healthy options on all of their menus and they have also imposed their own sugar tax. But come on, can he really get away with that? A chef selling steaks, burgers and molten chocolate praline pudding getting all evangelical about healthy food? This has to be a joke.

At the time of writing, the government look set to dilute many of their bold claims on a sugar tax and seem more keen to allow manufacturers and individuals to take responsibility. Jamie has been somewhat sidelined. And no bad thing. Still, during the entire period of Jamie popping up on telly every twelve seconds to lecture us on what's best for our heart valves, the value of Jamie's own group of companies increased once again and bookings for his restaurants continued to spiral ever northwards.

Maybe it's time to get back to basics and ditch the evangelical campaigning nonsense. How about *The Naked Chef 2*?

Jamie back in his kitchen getting all raw and groovy with grub again. Only this time the kitchen might be significantly larger, that small potted herb garden replaced by a few acres of lush land and the moped no doubt replaced by a shiny new Aston Martin. Compulsive viewing.

33.

EXOTIC PET OWNERS

'd found myself in a little greasy spoon round the back of Westminster. A fine little bolthole where on a good day you can clock all manner of heavyweight politicos stuffing their fizzogs with a full English before PMQs. It's not always a pretty picture. This was the place where I was about to meet Snake Boy.

For reasons unknown, I am a magnet for the eccentric and the mad. I'm not quite sure how or why this happens and I really can't trace when it first occurred, but if there's an oddball in the pub or a weirdo on the train, they tend to make a beeline in my direction. I've lost count of how many times I've been cornered or coerced into unrequited communication with a nutter. I'm a sucker for it and clearly my curious tendency to reciprocate is wholly to blame. While most people might just nod politely or force a smile, I, for some reason, get stuck into full-blown engagement. This clearly compounds an already awkward situation. I once spent the best part of two hours chatting to a man in the pub with a lampshade on his head. You get the idea.

My weirdo beacon was clearly giving off the vibes. A man wearing a beaten-up brown leather jacket with a florid complexion and shifty lips came and sat opposite me. Within seconds, the pleasantries were under way. Within a minute, I knew more about his life than I do of some of my mates. After five minutes, he'd ordered tea and a bun and was in full-on rant mode. Mark (named after Marc Bolan, he had informed me) wasn't going anywhere soon. He then took out his mobile phone in preparation for his big moment.

'Do you want to see something?' he said, teasingly. He waved away the clear look of concern that had shot across my face. 'This is my baby,' he said. He fired up his phone screen to show me a photo. He was clearly enjoying my manufactured look of anticipation. He nodded proudly as he flicked the screen in my direction. It was a *yep, it really is what you think*-type nod. He then put me out of my misery as he announced in deep-toned staccato what it was.

'Rare. Indian. Python.' He tapped the screen as he announced each word.

Mark was out to impress.

'An Indian python? Wow, incredible,' I said. Mark looked back at the screen and then to me.

'Where specifically are they found?' I asked.

Mark seemed confused by the question. He stared back at the image of his snake before eventually offering his considered response.

'Africa. I think.'

I hadn't wanted to make an immediate judgement on Mark but I guess I had. From the moment he'd sat down, I had assessed that he was probably a bit of an arse. Anyone who wears the kind of jacket that Huggy Bear would have discarded forty years previously was always going to be a wrong 'un.

But I had given him the benefit of the doubt and allowed him to join me. Isn't it only polite not to be too judgemental? I was now back to my original assessment.

'What do you feed it on?' I asked, like I gave a toss.

'The thing with ya python is that they have small stomachs. You're meant to buy those frozen rats and stuff – you can get them from the pet shops. But he doesn't seem to like them much. Maybe I'm not defrosting them properly…'

He paused for a second as he pondered his frozen rodent dilemma.

'…But to be honest, they'll eat anything. Scraps, chicken, carrots…'

Carrots? My knowledge of the snake is limited to those wildlife programmes and *The Jungle Book*. I'm clearly no authority on the palate of the python but I'm almost 100 per cent sure that they don't eat carrots. In fact, I'm *definitely* sure they don't eat them. Imagine how disappointing those Attenborough commentaries would be: 'The snake has spotted its prey. It remains still. And then, with lightning speed, it strikes. And with one super-fast constriction, the carrot is no more…'

Mark was out of his depth. He was clueless and bereft of any knowledge to do with his snake. And he's not alone. He's one of a growing number of oddballs who think that owning an exotic or wild animal is perfectly acceptable. From snakes and spiders through to monkeys and leopards, the list is disturbing. The UK is now home to millions of exotic pets. In 2014 alone, the animal reception centre at Heathrow saw over 200,000 reptiles pass through their gates. This is huge business and despite the underground and black market trade for these animals, most of it is legit. A quick Google search reveals that local authorities in the UK have licensed some curious beasts in the past few years:

- Aberdeenshire Council – 3 bison
- Calderdale Council – 2 rattlesnakes
- Bedford Borough Council – 2 grey wolves
- Boston Borough Council – 1 zebra
- Cannock Chase District Council – 3 tigers

To compound the confusion, the main concern from the councils appears to be safety rather than welfare. They don't seem to be that bothered if you want to keep a camel in your loft, just so long as it can't get out. You might have imagined that keeping any sort of wild and dangerous animals would require some kind of PhD in zoology, or at least some basic certification in animal husbandry. But it doesn't. So long as you can prove it won't escape, you're OK. You haven't got to be Dr Doolittle to know that monkeys and snakes are best kept in the forests of Africa or Asia, not in a semi-detached in Cleethorpes, but I guess if your core knowledge on these issues comes from Wikipedia, these kinds of petty facts just get in the way of owning a cool pet.

There's a Louis Theroux episode where he goes in search of a bunch of monkey-owning wackos down there in the Southern states. These people are off the scale, housing enormous collections of big cats and chimps with virtually zero knowledge about their needs and instincts. Every question he fires at them is met with either a blank stare or the kind of bumbled response you would expect from a six-year-old. It's tragic stuff.

The UK now boasts our very own version of these boneheads and they are growing in numbers.

Mark and his snake-owning cohorts are here to stay. The man at the stats office tells me that snakes and large spiders are two of the most common when it comes to private ownership. Their lifespan and well-being are dramatically reduced by being held in domestic conditions. But that doesn't matter to arse-clowns like Mark, who will go on kidding themselves that they have some kind of spiritual relationship with their pets and an insider knowledge of the animal kingdom. The reality couldn't be more different and people like him are the very kind who shouldn't be left in charge of a budgie, let alone an Indian python. The mere fact that certain humans actively desire to own an exotic pet should be the very reason that stops them from doing so.

My cuppa with the snake owner was short-lived. I made my excuses and left for work. Mark seemed perturbed by my hasty exit. I noticed that he never did eat that bun he ordered. Maybe my line of questioning had put him off his grub. Either that or he was planning on taking it home as a special treat for his pet elephant back in the prairies of Slough.

34.

PEOPLE WHO DON'T KNOW HOW TO EAT PROPERLY

At what point did we decide to dispense with knives when eating food? When did it become OK to eat an entire meal only with one hand and a fork? I'm almost sure this sloppy behaviour never used to happen.

I'm tempted to think that this somehow America's fault. The Yanks love a bit of casual eating. As distinct from some cultures, where a deep-rooted, almost holy, reverence is applied to food (the elixir of life etc.), our friends across the pond seem to have made eating an almost performance art. You haven't got to watch many movies to see that table etiquette plays little part in Uncle Sam's approach to food intake. As long as the stuff gets lobbed in there, it hardly matters whether that happens via a throw, a flick or even a catapult.

Us Brits always had a different approach. Perhaps post-war generations who appreciated the value of food, having lived through years of rationing, created a different type of respect for the way we all sit down to eat. Didn't every kid get taught how to hold a knife and fork nicely? Not to speak with their mouths full and – the big one – strictly no elbows on the table?

When did those three simple rules completely disappear from British life?

The elbows-on-the-table move now appears to be a national sport. This is pretty much the default position for swathes of Brits to adopt when tucking in: one arm casually resting in front of you and the other – with the elbow virtually glued to the table – stabbing away at the food. Not only does this break all of those nice polite conventions but isn't that stuck-elbow thing a bit impractical? Like riding a bike with your upper leg strapped to the crossbar? Use your damn arm, that's what it's there for.

Others take this nonchalant choreography a step further and go for the prison-eating approach. This is where you virtually stick your face into the plate by hunching right over the grub and simply scoop it in fork by fork at a rapid rate. I'm told there is a technical name for this: it's called eating like a fat pig. Were none of these oddballs ever taught *any* table manners?

Then there's the no-knife lot. This one is so spectacularly troubling that it almost slides into the arena of humour rather than something that should bother us all. I can't think of anything that is easier to eat without a knife rather than with one. But crazy Brits, in their new-found proclivity for casual eating, have decreed that the only time the knife might be picked up would be for self-defence purposes in the event of a potential dinner table mugging. Assuming that isn't going to be the case, the knife stays where it is. The upshot of this charade is that usually sane diners end up chasing food around their plates with a solo fork for almost the entirety of their meal; anything rather than pick up the bloody knife. Stabbing at troublesome tomatoes and attempting to harpoon a glazed carrot as they slide around the plate (and often *off* the plate) is all part of the no-knife experience, it seems. After several attempts at playing hockey with their scran, they invariably resort to using the tips of their fingers to guide the food back onto the fork. The fact that all this slippery mischief could be immediately addressed just by picking up that thing sitting right beside your plate seems lost on this bunch.

And then there's the money shot of cutlery crimes. This is where the offender attempts to use the fork as a knife. You don't need shares in Leatherman to know that the side of a fork is about as sharp as your own finger. It's completely useless when it comes to cutting. That's because it's a fork. This is clearly lost on our no-knife friends, who attempt to cut up all kinds of foodstuff from tough spuds to entire steaks using nothing more than the very blunt edge of their fork. Is it a challenge? Do they have some kind of cutlery dysmorphic disorder where they actually think it's a knife no matter hard they look at it?

I'm convinced that this slack approach to how we eat is relatively new. I'm pretty sure that when I was a kid in the '80s those little rules about elbows and cutlery were still very much in place. Maybe sitting nicely and eating properly have been removed from our templates of social normality under the auspices that tradition and good grace aren't particularly cool. Whatever is going on here, it's not unreasonable to point out that trying to cut up a beef Wellington with a fork is a very silly thing to do. A knife will do the job much better. I would even go so far as to say it's a game changer. It will also make your mum proud.

35.

SOCIAL MEDIA CAMPAIGNERS

It was the political coup of 2014 that you may not have even realised was happening. The Prime Minister, David Cameron, was about to be booted out of office.

There was to be an uprising. The people had spoken and they were *not* happy. Action needed to be taken. The premier had to go. He'll be gone by the end of the week, claimed one of the chief campaigners. This was clearly serious stuff and would surely be making international news. But it wasn't. Because it wasn't real. It was taking place in the parallel universe of social media.

The chosen method of unseating the Prime Minister wasn't what you might call classic coup style. There was to be no covert operation or underground meetings. There would be no Guevara-style recce to assess the political terrain and gauge the movements of the security forces. No one would need to paint their face, don a balaclava or spend hours in the gym getting revolution-fit. In fact, you didn't even have to get out of bed. David Cameron was to be removed from office and stripped of his prime ministerial powers by the use of… (drum roll) a hashtag.

Like all similar campaigns, it's almost impossible to find the person who started it. It doesn't really matter. What is beyond laughable is that any of these keyboard clowns thought it was going to work. For those who aren't familiar with Twitter and all of its linguistic foibles, the hashtag is invariably used to denote or abbreviate a view or opinion:

KFC is the best takeaway food on the god-darn planet. #TheColonelRules.

My local council forget to collect the bins again this week. #SortItOut

More recently, it's been used as a sort of collective way of show-ing acknowledgement of or even allegiance to a prominent news story or cause. All quite logical in the shorthand world of social media. Beyond that, it's kind of meaningless and certainly no serious person could believe that sticking a hashtag on your Twitter feed could get rid of a democratically elected PM. But the hashtag #CameronMustGo was intended to do exactly that. Not merely to cheekily highlight political disagreement or to bond with an online narrative about why the Tories are rotten. This was designed to actually unseat the man and those who posted, opined and retweeted really did believe that Cameron would be gone via the conduit of a symbol on Twitter. And, trust me, these clowns really *did* believe it.

After the first week of their campaign, I had lost count of the number of times I had clocked a post claiming 'We're nearly there' or 'Not long to go now' or 'Cameron must know it's over' – all accompanied by the requisite #CameronMustGo.

Curiously, the thrust of this 'campaign' wasn't based on a specific piece of legislation or policy. It wasn't driven by a definitive issue over the NHS or the government's refusal to scrap Trident. These were just people who didn't like Cameron. Essentially, people who didn't vote for the Conservatives. Which makes the logic even more baffling. An elected government should be unseated at will merely by dint of the fact that you didn't vote for them in the first place? Genius.

I couldn't take any more. I had to dive in. It's an error I don't often make on Twitter (I learnt long ago that unless you want your entire day – or week – taken up by parochial arguments and impenetrable logic, then best stay away), but this was getting silly. Time to dip my toe.

'Do you actually believe you are going to unseat a serving PM via Twitter?' I gently asked. I added the #CameronMustGo to ensure it hit the right places. It didn't take long before my entire existence (and parentage) was being questioned.

F*** off Collins, you Tory apologist #CameronMustGo

Wake up and smell the coffee Collins. You media elites know nothing #PeoplePower #CameronMustGo

Over 100,000 people can't be wrong. Watch this space. #CameronMustGo #Bastard

The Tory apologist thing was a bit of a low blow. I hadn't shown any political allegiance, merely questioned the logic of the campaign. The 'media elite' thing is a common one hurled by halfwits at folk who just happen to have a job in media.

But it was the number thing that was interesting. One hundred thousand people is impressive, but is it *real*? What does it actually mean?

The contemporary world of tech has completely recalibrated the way we function, and that includes the arena of protest and dissent. But how do we quantify this change? One hundred and twenty-four thousand people voted for a vessel to be called Boaty McBoatface, 3.5 million people voted for Craig the chippy to win *Big Brother* and half a million people joined in the online frenzy of knocking an *X Factor* winner off the top of the charts by purchasing a Rage Against the Machine track. Big numbers are not always the currency of kudos or rationale. They are just big numbers and they can be arrived at in all kinds of ways. The penchant for registering disquiet, approval or appetite for an idea or notion via a tweet, a cut and pasted post or a button on your remote is certainly here to stay but does it seriously authenticate anything? I can't imagine anyone really believes that 100k keyboard warriors hitting retweet to get rid of Cameron carries the same weight of credibility as tens of thousands of suffragettes taking to the streets of London and getting knocked around by the Old Bill for their troubles.

Predictably, the #CameronMustGo campaign quickly descended into a #CameronNeverDidGo situation. It was always a bonkers idea. If you ask enough people at any random point in time 'Do you think the government is a bit shit?', about 90 per cent of people will say yes, but we don't then arrange an impromptu general election on the front lawn to reflect that. In any case, it's surely a loaded question: don't we *always* think governments are a bit shit? If you place that question into the echo chamber that is Twitter and ask your followers to retweet to all of *their* followers, all will dutifully oblige. To achieve 100,000 *anything* on Twitter isn't that difficult – mathematically it doesn't take that many stages of retweeting to achieve the aim. But beyond the numbers, what the hell is the point? The whole 'campaign' merely becomes a self-serving circular exercise that achieves sod all.

Hashtags have a place and they have a point, but the idea that a bunch of dozy sofa monkeys could use one to remove a Prime Minister from office was always ridiculous. Tragically, this lot really did think it would work. So, a word of advice for any wannabe protesters: instead of mooching around your flat plotting political rebellion via your index finger, take a leaf out of the books of King and Pankhurst: knock up some decent placards, mobilise a million *real* people and get your arses out there and makes some damn noise. #LazyGits

36.

CRYPTIC FACEBOOK POSTERS

This one has been driving me around the pipe for years. You log onto Facebook and one of your 'friends' has posted this:

I can't believe this is happening to me

Cripes. Have they been kidnapped? Did they manage to swiftly post a status update before being loaded into the boot of a car? Or have they accidentally OD'd on echinacea after misreading the RDA? Or perhaps they have just discovered that their mum and dad are not their biological parents but adopted them some years back from George and Laura Bush?

Or is it good news? Have they won the lottery, just been hired on a six-figure salary or maybe just opened the front door to see Orlando Bloom stood there naked with a bunch of flowers in his hands?

'I can't believe this is happening' clearly suggests drama – of some kind. You check their previous post. The last one, from the night before, yields no clues: 'Having a night out with mates. Hello Manchester.' I suppose there could be a connection. Maybe it's a hangover post – 'I can't believe this is happening' could be referring to the Monday morning blues after too much ale had been supped in the fine bars of Deansgate. But it doesn't *sound* like one of those. Surely 'Hungover – can't believe I have to work' would do the trick. The post is confusing. And worrying.

It doesn't take long before fellow friends launch into action: 'What's wrong?', 'Hope nothing bad is happening', 'Can you let us know you're all right?' etc. There are maybe twenty of these replies. And still nothing. 'I can't believe this is happening to me' remains unanswered. This isn't looking good. You start to think the unthinkable; perhaps this will be the last we ever hear from our friend. In years to come, we'll all remember and discuss those last haunting words. Once in a while a TV crew will rock up to retell the story and we'll all be asked to give our theories about what we think might have taken place.

Fifteen minutes later and the drama has intensified: 'Please, we need to know you're OK', 'I tried to text you but got no reply', 'You sound so distressed'. There are now over fifty posts, all with the same concerns.

Finally, after an hour, our friend is back on. She's alive!

'Sorry guys, was just having a bad morning. Slept through alarm, no hot water, late for work. BF not talking to me.'

You utter arse. At what point did you think it was OK to post a random sentence like that? Was there not a moment when you thought it might just look a little bit sinister? Did you not consider that half your mates might be worried out of their skins? You can't have *not* known how that sentence might have read to others? In any case, if you wanted to impart the doom-based nature of your day so far, then why didn't you just say what you said in the second post to begin with?

The cryptic post is all too common. And deliberate. An attention-seeking way of galvanising mass concern about the person's well-being or predicament, and then sitting back and watching the ensuing chaos. Even the more innocuous posts: 'I've just made the biggest mistake of my life' and 'It's not looking good for me' (two recent ones I spotted) are clearly written for the same self-indulgent and deluded reasons. A way of getting others to ask and enquire about their intriguing life. So a polite word to those drama monkeys of social media: it's not meant to be a quiz where your friends have to guess your current predicament. If you have something to say, just spit it out.

This is just another example of how Facebook & Co. have changed the way we function. Just when you think common sense or tact might override stupidity, up it crops again. Remember the rule of thumb: if you wouldn't say it or do it in the real world then it's probably advisable that you shouldn't do so in the virtual one either.

So next time you wake up with the hump and you want to impart your angst onto Facebook, then quit with the cryptic lark and tell it like it is. That way all your friends won't be gearing up to speed-dial *Crimewatch* while trying to muster up personalised obituaries about what an amazing person you once (apparently) were.

37.

AMATEUR TRAFFIC WARDENS

In the very busy world of people doing stupid things, competition is pretty fierce. Remember, this book is the unequivocal Bible of annoying stuff. Yet despite my forthright proclamation on this point, I am more than aware that we might have some disagreement in the ranks. My own family and friends stand to fall out with me on several. I understand subjectivity but I am just a bit disappointed with it. As a way of making sure we can all be friends, let's throw in another contender where there really can be no grey areas, where the collective brains of Hans Blix and Michael Mansfield couldn't proffer a reservation or defence.

Thatcher called it personal responsibility, Blair went with social responsibility and Cameron referred to it as the Big Society, but it all amounted to the same thing: men, women and nippers alike all doing their bit to make the community a better place. Don't wait for the man from the council to pick up the litter; if you see it, do it yourself. It's your patch, so have some pride, for God's sake. Without individuals doing their bit, there's zero chance of achieving the wider aim of a civilised and cohesive society. It all begins with the individual.

But nowhere within the philosophical ideals of our great leaders does it suggest that part of being an active citizen involves pretending to be a traffic warden and gluing parking tickets onto the windscreens of your neighbours' cars, just because you're a bit pissed off that they parked outside your house. I don't recall seeing that in any manifesto.

I've experienced this brain ache on three distinct occasions.

'You can't leave your car there.' The man was in his mid-twenties. He was very unhappy.

'Why not? – it's a road,' I countered, with the reasonableness of a very reasonable man.

'But it's in front of our house.' His eyes widened as he pointed first at my car and then back to his house, as if somehow I was unaware of which two things he was referring to.

'Yes, it is.'

'You can't park there.'

'Why?'

'Because it's front of our house.' He looked at me as if I had just parked my car in his front room.

How the hell do you come back from that? I was trying to work out if there was a way to visually impart the word knobhead solely via the conduit of a single facial expression. He was clearly having the same thought. The stand-off was only broken when a woman – presumably his mother – came out of the house wailing. She really *was* wailing.

'Why are you doing this to us?' said the mad mother, waving her arms all over the show. Leaping lizards. Is she having some sort of attack?

'See, you've upset my mother now. You can't park here. We put a sign on your car to tell you this.'

He had indeed put a sign on my car. An entire sheet of A3 paper taped to the back window with the scribbled message 'This is not a dumping ground for your car. Please move it.' So that I didn't feel too singled out, he'd also placed an identical sign on the car parked behind me. This man was clearly bat-shit crazy. His mother continued to wave and wail while Matey stood firm with his arms folded and the face of a man who was about to carry out some kind of martial arts manoeuvre on my head. To compound the unfathomable nature of this scenario, the guy had a driveway – a bigger than average, beautifully stone-clad, shiny driveway. With two cars parked on it. He just hated the idea that anyone would park outside his house. I pointed out that there were no bays, no road markings and no regulations about who can park where. I pointed to my own house to show that there was someone parked outside mine too. This is just the way it is, I had said – it's a busy road and people tend to park where they can. Ideally, we would all love to park right outside our own front door but this isn't always possible. Even strangers can legitimately park here, it's a free road. I pleaded my unarguable point. He was having none of it.

'If I have to, I will go to the council, or the police.'

Man alive, this gets worse. I tried to imagine the court case. What would I be charged with, geographical tarmac abuse? I could see the judge donning his black cap, explaining in sombre tones that my existence was to be snuffed out for parking my Mini Cooper in a thoughtless manner outside No. 67 Woodlands Way.

'Mate, it's a public road – which bit of that do you not get? Anyone can park here. Whenever they like – this isn't your parking space. It's a public road.'

'You are everything that is wrong with this country. How do you sleep at night?' He shook his head like he was arguing with a sex offender.

I wanted to hammer down into the deepest levels of his mad psychology. Do people like this *actually* exist? When he lays his head on the pillow at night will he *really* believe that he was in the right? But I knew the battle was lost. He had more than made up his mind and whatever logic I was about to throw his way would be batted away with the same impervious guff.

A couple of years back, having parked my car perfectly legally on a vacant piece of concrete, I was approach by a man in his sixties. He had the air of a military type – an important walk, a fixed scowl and a copy of the *Daily Mail* under his arm.

'What's going on here then?' asked the man in the tweed jacket.

'Er, nothing,' I said. 'Just parking my car.'

He ingested some air as he pondered my utterly ridiculous reply.

'Right, we can deal with this one of two ways, Sonny Jim.' He pointed towards my tyres and gestured a kind of mad knifing action as he delivered the ultimatum. Flipping heck, a *Daily Mail*-reading pensioner was threatening to slash my tyres.

'But I'm allowed to park here. It's a public road,' I stated evenly.

'No, you're not, this is my house and you can't park here. Now dick off.'

Dick off? Nobody had ever told me to *dick* off before. Is that an actual thing – a real insult? Either way, the Colonel wasn't happy and he was standing firm. I wondered what his reaction would have been had he read a story in his *Daily Mail* about errant yobs slashing up people's tyres (and then telling them to dick off). This man had hang 'em and flog 'em dripping from every pore. Yet here he was threatening me with a knife attack on my finest Dunlops.

The upshot was that I managed to stare out this old fart for a good thirty seconds before nonchalantly walking off. I wasn't about to let military smugness and bully-boy tactics win the day; I needed to make a stand. As I got to the end of the road, I hid behind a Ford Mondeo and waited for him to re-enter his house (presumably to fetch a recently sharpened Sabatier). As soon as I heard his door shut, I legged it back to my car and *dicked off* up the road like lightning. You can't be too sure.

Where I live now, one belligerent old harridan has got so angry about motorists parking in a completely legal and legitimate manner that she has taken to making her own parking tickets. Anyone who dares to darken her doorstep (or about half a mile either side) with four wheels will almost certainly be on the receiving end of one of her tailor-made tickets. From what we can work out, she has three versions. One explains that this is a residents' only area and nobody but a resident can park there (not true). Another says that the cars are parked on a dangerous blind spot and will cause an accident (not true) and the other points out that cars are causing an obstruction for emergency vehicles (not true). On each note she informs the driver that photographic evidence has been collated and the police have been informed. Each little ticket is then placed into a small 4x4 cm polythene bag (which presumably she had to specifically source from somewhere) and taped to the windscreen of the offending vehicle. She then spends the best part of the day twitching her own net curtains watching confused drivers reading her bogus tickets before screwing them up and lobbing them into the nearest garden (ironically, usually hers). She never actually sees any benefit or consequence from this bizarre ritual other than, one presumes, a zillion ulcers floating around in her sizeable torso as a result of tying herself into complete knots over something that *isn't* actually happening.

We all know that parking is tricky these days and getting space can be a complete ball-ache. We've all endured that walk of doom when you had to park your car about eight miles from your own house. But it's swings and roundabouts and the next day you get the space and someone else has to virtually hail a cab home.

So who are the self-appointed traffic fascists? Is it a missing chromosome? A learnt behaviour? Or just a general disposition of misery and angst? I asked this question on the radio, genuinely interested to see if there was some kind of psychology paper out there that could shine some light. It appears no one, thus far, has dipped their toe into this particular pool. That said, I had an email from Mike in Bradford who advised me to give up my quest for an explanation. He made the very reasonable point that if social anthropologists have yet to work out why some people enjoy Morris dancing or set an alarm for 5 a.m. in order to go jogging, then we're unlikely to solve this one either. It's a fair point. The parking Gestapo are going nowhere.

38.

CORBYN AND FARAGE SUPER-FANS

Here's a representation of an email I have received about 200 times.

Collins

Can you ever leave it alone? We are not interested in your views on Nigel/Jeremy. Keep them to yourself. If you can't be nice, then don't say anything. Nigel/Jeremy is a breath of fresh air. He represents real people – not just the rich and privileged. Who are you to constantly give him a hard time? He has more humanity in his little finger than you have in your entire body. You and the rest of the media are constantly having a pop. We are NOT interested in your opinion. Nigel/Jeremy understands what is going on out there and will change things for the good. He will help the real people, not just the bankers and the rich. Nigel/Jeremy wants a fairer Britain and he will rebuild the country. That's because he cares. You have no right to constantly criticise him. It's getting boring now. Leave him alone!

Bodger McGoo

Let's break this down. Hosting a nightly phone-in show inevitably means that our political masters and their daily endeavours feature regularly on the menu – it's the very core of the agenda. Having a fairly robust (and often brutal) take on Westminster's finest is all part of the deal. And let's be honest, British politicians really are the gift that keeps on giving. Whether it's Hilary Benn and Harriet Harman for Labour or Michael Fallon and Amber Rudd for the Tories (and every Lib Dem and SNP bod in between), nobody seems too fussed by a national lampooning of the girls and boys from the green benches. With two exceptions.

Nigel Farage and Jeremy Corbyn have identical types of super-fan. And *fan* is the word. Whatever the story or debate, the moment I launch into a 'the trouble with Nigel/Jeremy' rant, Team Farage or Team Corbyn go apoplectic. The phone lines explode, Twitter launches into action and weird variants of the above email start to glide into my inbox.

There are clearly very few obvious parallels to be drawn between Nigel and Jeremy. That said, there is some commonality in terms of their backgrounds. Both had an extremely privileged upbringing, both went to private schools and both are worth more than a few quid. They also share the status of having a Christian name that might be better placed on a theatre poster than in the corridors of power. But politically they couldn't be further apart. One left and one right. Yet both of these very different politicians are able to command identical and inexplicable levels of messianic worship from their respective fans.

The core case against me when it comes to having a pop at this pair appears to be based on an alarmingly stupid premise: they are good people and therefore I have no right to attack them. Genius. What is this, North Korea? These are people who actively desire ultimate power; they believe they possess an inner wisdom that needs to be wheeled out for the common good. Surely these are the *very* types of people who should be regularly dragged into the spotlight for some brutal analysis?

'But he wants to make a difference,' cry the Nigel/Jerry massive. Balls. I've never met a politician who *didn't* want to make a difference. They might have varying ways of going about it (this pair are surely the greatest case in point), but all harbour the same vainglorious belief in their ability to make the world a better place. Anyone who possesses those levels of self-confidence should rightly be up for as much scrutiny, doubt and even ridicule as one can muster.

'Leave him alone, he's doesn't deserve this.' Man alive, I'm not talking about your dad. Any protection he might have had from a public lashing ended the moment he stuck his name on the ballot paper. The day we have to stop having a pop at our political masters – based on nothing more than the wonky hypothesis that it might upset them – is the day we all pack up and go home.

'It's a media conspiracy.' No, it isn't. Both of these men, in differing ways, have become massive headlines over the past few years. Their narratives, their policies and even their characters are game-changing in the world of politics. Don't be surprised when you see that disproportionately covered in some of the press. Both of these men sit in far more extreme areas of the political spectrum than we have been used to in mainstream politics, so it stands to reason that the media (as if that's one giant entity) will be far more inclined to dig a little deeper when it comes to exposing or contradicting their backgrounds and politics.

'He's a better person than you.' Good God, how old are you, six? Maybe he is, maybe he isn't; quit the territorial stuff – you can't take ownership of these people. This is politics, not *Britain's Got Talent*.

As I'm writing this, a woman called Ruth has just kicked off on Twitter:

> @IanCollinsUK: Collins you shouldn't be attacking Jeremy, you should be helping him. He wants to make the world a better place.

And there we go again. I should be helping him, like it's a settled view that he is right in the first place? And that's the issue. These guys simply cannot get beyond the delusional belief that there could be another opinion out there. Any attempt to highlight this fairly obvious point is dismissed with the same levels of anger you would normally reserve for someone who has just kicked your cat.

For what it's worth, I've met both Nigel and Jeremy. Two curious men: one wishes it was 1876 and the other 1976. My own assessment is that both are a bit charming, both have massive egos and both are a bit weird. Neither, however, are about to become the next Churchill or Bevan. So give yourself a break, *Corage* fans. Your idols will be gone soon, consigned to the political dustbin alongside the likes of John Prescott and Norman Lamont. All political careers ultimately end in failure; right now Jezza and Nige are heading that way with impressive speed.

39.

BACKPACKERS

There are two types of people who go backpacking. Those who travel the world to take in the impressive and awe-inspiring sights and cultures of multiple countries and to educate themselves that there's more to life than *EastEnders* and Nandos. And then there's Spencer and his friends.

When I was eighteen, I got one of those summer jobs down in Spain. Usual drill: low pay, room thrown in and a gig that involved looking after several hundred sun-worshipping tourists who would arrive by the truckload on a weekly basis. It was all a bit route one but I didn't care, I was a kid in the sunshine having fun. I was staying just a stone's throw from a place called Mijas, a quiet and quaint village that sat in the hills of Andalusia. This place was old school and completely untouched by the hands of chip-eating Brits. Speaking English in Mijas was not an option, crazy fun pubs were non-existent and if you asked where you could buy sunscreen, you would have been hounded out of the village. This place was Spain circa 1952, where locals really did still walk through the dusty streets with donkeys and widows wore black.

For one reason or another, I ended up spending a fair

amount of time there. It was a learning curve and a life-changer. I'd got to know one or two local families who, for whatever reason, seemed quite taken by this youthful, pasty Brit. Consequently, I spent more than the odd evening with a couple of the bar owners and their families, who took a proud delight in regaling me with tales and tribulations from the good old days. They spoke with huge gestures and big smiles as they reminisced their way through the decades. I would smile back, understanding virtually none of it but sort of getting the gist. Sometimes the smiles would turn to sadness as they predicted an inevitable encroachment on their land from golf courses and holiday apartments (more than prophetic, as it turned out). As the vino flowed, they would play music, talk flamenco and food, and explain why bullfighting really wasn't such a bad thing; Mijas boasted the only *square* bullring in Spain, something they were fiercely proud of. As the nights came to an end, several carafes of wine and packs of Fortunas later, I would say goodbye, the old toothless grandmother – the matriarch of the piece, sitting sagely in her old wicker chair – would blow a little kiss, and I'd be off, back down the hill to the other world. Until the next time.

I was on the verge of telling an abridged version of this story to a posh bloke called Spencer at a house party in Kent. He'd asked me if I had ever 'been travelling'. I kind of knew where this was going.

'Yeah, spent six months in Spain a few years ago…' I began.

That's as far as it got. Spencer and his uni mate pretty much hit the deck. For some reason this was the funniest thing anyone had said to them for years.

'*Spain?*' said Spencer, as if I had just said Mars. '*Spain?*'

he repeated. 'That doesn't really count does it? I mean, come on...'

'That's kind of pretty standard. Not really travelling, is it...?' added his twat of a mate.

'Yeah, hardly Thailand,' said Spencer.

I smiled. But I wanted to lump him one.

'So you've been to Thailand?' I asked, because I couldn't think of anything else to say.

This was the cue for Spencer and his mates to combust some more.

'Have I been to Thailand?' he asked back. Spencer turned to his mate.

'Rufus, have I been to Thailand?' he said rhetorically, with a grin that made him look like someone holding in wind.

'Er, yes, just for the eight whole weeks,' said Rufus, as if confirming his mate's status as pretty much the Thai ambassador.

This wasn't the first time I had stumbled across this mucked-up logic. Who knew that there was such a pecking order in the world of travel – a league table of authentic experience based on nothing more than distance? If you haven't *done* India or Thailand and maybe a bit of Oz, then somehow you are an incomplete human in the world of travel. Monkeying around in Spain with some wrinkled-up Latinos doesn't make the grade. It's not far enough away.

I couldn't be bothered to tell Spencer and Rufus that I had, in fact, been to most of these 'real' places multiple times. I wanted to drill down a bit on just how cultured his global endeavours had been. I had a hunch that he and his buddy hadn't exactly been meditating with the Buddhist monks of Chiang Rai.

'So, how was Thailand?' I asked.

'Man, it was madness.'

He was puckering up for a killer story. It was clearly going to be rubbish.

'I have never drunk that much in my life. We were pissed pretty much from the moment we jumped on the plane to the moment we got back on it. Must have gone to about 200 different beach parties. If you want a proper trip, I'm telling you – Thailand every time.'

Him and Rufus then did a weird salute thing with their beer bottles and made a chesty, tribal grunt. Obviously some kind of ritual thing they'd come up with as a show of their shared Thai experience. Dicks.

'So, is that all you did, then – get pissed?' I asked.

'Pretty much, apart from the last week. Had a bit of a coach trip thing. Got dropped off at the Khao San Road – even had a KFC – and got bladdered with a bunch of Europeans. Smoked the best gear ever and shagged the waitress.'

Blimey, he should have just gone to Bromley.

'Tell him about the guy outside the bar,' said Rufus.

'Mental. Got talking to this local guy on the street. Really nice bloke, spoke fluent English – supported Man United and stuff – and told me about a few bars up the road where they let you smoke a bit of weed and nobody bothers you. Went back inside to tell this one about it…' he nodded towards Rufus '… and realised the little bastard had robbed me blind. Everything gone: wallet, passport, phone, the lot…'

Again, should have gone to Bromley.

Spencer could hardly believe the brilliance of his own story. He'd spent three grand and travelled 6,000 miles, essentially to get pissed. He hadn't 'been travelling' – he'd simply left point A on a map and went to point B. But, in his world, the fact that these shenanigans happened in Bangkok and not Benidorm somehow cemented his status as a seasoned traveller who now had some kind of virtuous hold over those who hadn't made such an audacious trip.

So when some bonehead starts waxing lyrical about how they have *been travelling* – check their credentials. If they haven't swum in the Ganges, been run over by an elephant in Nairobi or pooped in a cave in Pattaya, then the chances are they haven't really been travelling, they've just been on holiday.

40.

FANCY DRESS ADDICTS

It said on the invitation that fancy dress was optional. Thank the Lord. Despite it being the twenty-first century, where the list of stuff that can keep us human folk occupied seems never-ending, dressing up in amusing clothes still constitutes some sort of social highlight for a select few. Personally, I'd rather stick my fingers in a food blender. Turning up at my mate's house and seeing him dressed as Little Bo Peep was not a good start to the evening. I was immediately overwhelmed by a desire to vomit over his dress. I held it back.

'What's up with you, man? Where's your gear?' said Mike, wearing his bonnet.

'I decided to exercise the optional option,' I said.

As we walked into the house, I could hear the beat of music coming from the front room. A thousand horrors were about to be unleashed.

This was probably about the fifth time in my life that I had found myself at a fancy dress party. It was also the fifth time that I had no fancy dress. We live in a marvellous democracy and if some people feel that an evening is immeasurably enhanced by lobbing on some clothes and dressing up as someone else, then fine by me. I just resent the idea that I am the one with the problem if I opt not to do so. I've yet to nail the correlation between fancy dress and added fun.

When you're a kid, this kind of stuff *is* fun. It's more than fun – it's a highlight. The dressing-up box at school was arguably the most mesmerising and exciting item in the entire classroom. But, like all phases we go through while growing up – using a dummy, climbing trees and watching *Blue Peter* – there comes a point when you realise the appeal has waned, consigned to that beautiful box marked childhood memories. I was pondering this thought as I made the walk of doom through Mike's hallway, wondering what it is that changes within us and suddenly makes us disinterested in all the things that were once so magical. But then I remembered I had the answer. You become a fricking adult. That'll be why. The desire to stick on some rubber pants and pretend to be Batman no longer has quite the same appeal as when I was eight. All rather simple.

Yet across the land, week in and week out, fully matured human beings decide that the optimum way to pass a Saturday evening is to grab some old britches and hats and dress up as notable figures.

As Mike opened the sitting-room door, the grim enormity of the event was revealed. In the far corner a man waggled an oversized cigar in my direction (Harpo Marx, I guess); there was a woman with little ears and whiskers (Catgirl, maybe) and a fella standing in some sort of dustbin that hung from his shoulder by braces (not sure if he was a very bad Dusty Bin or a terrible R2D2, but either way, he seemed very happy). I spotted a Frankenstein, a Dracula, an Austrian mountain girl and a nun. The Blues Brothers on the sofa kicked off an im-promptu chant of 'Killjoy' aimed at my clear lack of effort. I then spent the next hour attempting to see through greasepaint and false beards trying to establish if I actually knew any of these people.

I couldn't help but wonder if Mike's menagerie of celebrity doppelgängers were *really* that happy. I wondered if there was some kind of deep-rooted psychological explanation for all of this. Does it fall somewhere into the category of fetish – a weird infantilising of oneself to procure a social ease? And how do they quantify this alleged fun? If I drink too much, I can tangibly gauge my mood based on a *feeling*. If I dance like a loon all night, little chemicals will start bolting around my brain and increase my smile factor. But if I stick a pair of elephant ears on my head, aside from looking like a bit of a tit, does something *happen*? Do I get a neurological return on my investment? In any case, isn't it all a bit of a ball-ache? Over in the corner there's a Roman centurion who can hardly move for body armour. Surely not conducive to a relaxing night out.

Whatever the motivations behind this curious ritual, this lot seemed content in their new skins. I was more than OK in my real one. I had a few drinks and began to leave. I said goodbye to Stevie Wonder and nodded farewell to Tony Blair. The wackiness was sending me over the edge. Time to go. As I was walking out, Timmy Mallett pitched up.

'You look like you could be a serial killer,' he said, pointing out my black overcoat and leather gloves. He poked his tongue out, Mallett-style, and giggled, blissfully unaware of how pro-phetic his suggestion might just become. I gave him my best Hannibal stare and buggered off.

41.

MAGISTRATES

Who needs an Xbox? One episode of *Road Wars* and every boy's dream of an off-the-scale alternative reality is totally fulfilled – with lights on. Big-ass blue flashing lights.

Road Wars airs on various satellite and cable channels. If you flick between them regularly enough, it's virtually on a 24-hour loop. It follows the Thames Valley Police proactive unit. These are the undercover guys who patrol the streets of Reading looking for all manner of antisocial dodgepots and criminal activity. Drugs, theft and car crime are all on the menu as Pat & Karl, Simon & Yorkie, Rosie & Daz take to the highways in order to scoop up the lowlifes and keep them streets nice and clean. And when these fellas stick their foot on the gas, I'm there with them every step of the way. It is crucial to note that *Road Wars* is best viewed solo while in a sitting position. Just imagine your armchair is the back of a police car. Enjoy the ride.

But there's a problem. *Road Wars* throws up a pretty fundamental question from the off: what in the name of Gene Hunt do you have to do to be sent to prison in this country? A day in the life of the boys and girls in blue demonstrates the point.

We've just taken a call from Sarge. A couple of Herberts have nicked a car and are giving it large around the estate. Daz fires up the engine. We're off. We're following a stolen Ford Escort and they've already gained some ground. Rosie radios through the commentary: 'Left left left onto Meades Avenue – two white males, neither wearing seat belts. Over.' They're a good half a mile away. Daz shifts into fourth as we hit several speed humps at a tasty sixty. I find myself tilting at forty-five degrees as we take a particularly tricky bend on the Ridings Estate. I knew I was in for the long haul. We've narrowed the chase and are now virtually kissing the bumper of the knackered Escort. Sadly, Dumb and Dumber have a plan. They've employed a technique straight out of the trusty handbook of criminal knobheadery: if things are looking dodgy on the road, simply drive on the path. The Escort mounts the kerb and narrowly misses a young mum with a pushchair. Disbelief. It then tears through a playing field where several kids are gathered.

Meanwhile, back on the sofa, it's all sweat and tension. I catch my own reflection in the TV screen; my eyeballs appear to have left my head. Back on the road it's only a matter of time. The Escort has taken out several parked cars along the way. But with a row of concrete bollards up ahead, this can only end one way. A series of thuds and prangs signifies the end game. Rosie and Daz are out of the car with the speed of a pair of *Avengers* characters. With a single shout of 'You're a racist' (from the white kid to the white officer), it's all over. They're cuffed, bundled and taken down to the station. Result.

So what kind of punishment do you get for stealing a car, speeding, jumping several red lights, mounting the kerb, wrecking eight cars, nearly killing seventeen school kids, not wearing your seat belt, having no licence and being in possession of three grams of Colombia's finest? Go on, have a guess. Five years in the chiller? Three years and a five grand fine? Think again. This pair of chancers were fined £250 and given six points on their non-existent licences. That's less than a parking ticket in Camden. Who's running our judiciary – Keith Lemon?

I appreciate that magistrates are not quite the same legal deal as their ermine-clad brothers in the Crown Courts but they do still have the power to impose hefty fines and even prison. If in doubt, they can always refer a case to a higher court. Yet time after time road-based idiocy like this is virtually ignored by the very body that could do something about it. We send people to jail in this country for not paying a TV licence, we imprison ramblers who choose to go about their business naked, yet the response from magistrates for driving offences on this kind of scale is lamentable.

Simon & Yorkie have just stumbled across this genius...

Copper: So, is it your car?

Crim: No, it's my brother's.

Copper: What's your name?

Crim: David Mayhew.

Copper: What's your brother's name?

Crim: Er, David Mayhew.

Copper: But you said that's your name.

Crim: Yes, we have the same name.

Copper: You're not telling us the truth, are you?

Crim: Yes, I am.

These boys deal with this level of abject stupidity 24/7. Daft denials and outright BS are the order of the day. Again, the fine is ridiculous – £200 and a few penalty points for nicking a car and driving without a licence. Dave looks relieved and half the nation's criminal fraternity have just laughed their baseball caps off. *Road Wars* is beginning to look like a price list of risk for the criminally active.

Magistrates are missing a huge trick. At the time of writing I was unable to locate any data as to how many of them have ever actually watched an episode of *Road Wars*. They need to give it a go – sharpish. Given the amount of TV airtime that cop and car shows get, this would surely be a pivotal opportunity to educate the judiciary in the ways and means of Britain's four-wheeled arse-clowns and their calamitous endeavours. Perhaps they would then understand the futility of their current sentencing policies and realise that a massive austere kick up the patootie in the form of large fines and years in jail has to be the way forward. It's also a perfect opportunity to refuel the public coffers from the proceeds of such idiocy.

If nothing else, they can just enjoy the best darn cop show on TV. For those who have yet to experience the heart-stopping delights of Thames Valley's finest, I urge you to give it a go. Grab some popcorn and fizzy pop and buckle in. I promise you, a few episodes of *Road Wars* makes Call of Duty feel like a session of Pong.

42.

MEN WHO SHOW UP AT PARTIES WITH A GUITAR

When I was about eighteen, I was invited to a house party by an older mate called Len. He was twenty-five. He had an older mate called Trevor, who was thirty-five. All of Trevor's mates were between thirty-five and forty. And most of them were at the party. My chief memory of that terrible night is not just that I was eighteen and stuck in a room full of people whose average was about thirty-eight (essentially, like going out with your mum and dad) but that Trevor whipped out a guitar and started singing 'Here Comes the Sun'. I was stunned. Why would he want to do this?

'...Little Darling...'

Shit. I need to get out.

I vowed never to go to a house party again that contained anyone over the age of thirty-five. This lot were bonkers. They had these mad conversations about ISAs and kids. They discussed pilates and the cost of railway season tickets. And they all seemed to harbour an odd desire to own more than one house. On top of that, some of them showed up with guitars. This was a demographic that needed to be avoided.

And then I became thirty-five.

By thirty-five, house parties take on a slightly different vibe. For a start, they often begin at half two in the afternoon and finish by about six. Not good. Half the room aren't drinking because they've got kids and need to drive, those who used to smoke a bit of weed have given it up in the name of whatever the latest health craze might be, and the music choice becomes decidedly retro. Nowt wrong with a bit of Bananarama, I suppose. And then there's this guitar thing. What's all that about? Why the desire to entertain? You wouldn't pitch up with a magic show and start producing rabbits out of socks – people would just think you'd gone mad. So why the chronic need to play the guitar? And with what kind of levels of unbridled self-confidence do you have to muster up to think that a room full of people (many of whom you probably won't know) want to hear you banging out tunes of yesteryear in the name of family-based entertainment? Who but an utter cock-womble would think that was OK?

'Shall I get old Susie out?' says our man with the plectrum.

Old Susie? Man alive, he's even got a bloody name for it. Isn't that like people who name their cars? People you just want to smack in the kisser?

Out comes Susie. Guitar Boy is among friends. Clearly not everyone is sharing my bilious sense of impending doom. I can see some smiling faces. I think we have other singers in the ranks. He's off.

'What would you do if I sang out of tune…'

What is it with Beatles songs? Is that all they show you on the 'Teach yourself to play the guitar so that you can show up at a mate's house party and starting playing without anyone actually asking you to do so' YouTube channel? The chorus is nearing…

'Oh, I get by with a little help from my friends…'

Big smiles all round and a few giggles from the lads. One of them is tapping his foot in a slightly overambitious manner, getting the beat going.

'Mm, I get high with a little help from my friends…'

By this stage our man with the guitar is squinting like he's Bob Dylan. He's got right into this. A couple of the chorus boys are beckoning the rest of us to join in. If I wanted a sing-a-long, I'd have booked to see Barry Manilow. I've come round to a mate's for a few beers and to chew the fat, yet here I am being implored to sing a song. We all smile politely as we continue to watch the gig.

'…Mm, gonna try with a little help from my friends…'

As he gets to the end of the track, he does a bit of stringed improv thing to bring the song to a far more dramatic conclusion than John and Paul ever intended. He then hits the body of the guitar twice to signify that track one is done. Claps all round and a short break before launching into 'Hey Jude'.

Some sage advice for anyone under the age of about twenty-four. When you do hit your mid-thirties, only accept party invites from all your younger mates and resign yourself to being the slightly annoying older person. At all costs, avoid any kind of shindig within your own age group, just in case the guitar demon ramps up. Believe me, it's the lesser of two evils.

43.

SELFIE STICKERS

I'm pretty sure the entire nation had the same thought. When I first heard about something called the selfie stick, I assumed it was a joke. Like one of those fake ads from *Viz* selling 'central heating in a can' and 'altar boy chastity pants'.

A mate of mine had been in Edinburgh and was explaining how he had seen a man standing on North Bridge taking photos of himself with his mobile phone attached to a massive stick. Nothing about this sounded right. There was no frame of reference here. I couldn't muster up a mental picture of what that might look like or how it would work. How do you attach your phone to a stick, for a start? And who the hell would stand in a public place holding one of these things and not feel like a bit of a turnip? Surely this had to be some kind of publicity thing to promote one of the shows for the festival? But it wasn't. It was real.

For some of our fellow humans, carrying a selfie stick now appears to be as normal as carrying an umbrella. The lightning speed at which it has become just another part of contemporary life is astonishing; it's more than telling that when you do spot one of these loons standing in a very public place pointing an extendable rod towards the stars, nobody seems to blink. Myself and my radio producer Alex were watching a sea of tourists in Leicester Square, pondering this very point. As we stared out of our studio window, we counted over twenty of these stick monkeys all going nuts for the ultimate snap. One man had taken it a step further. He'd taped two sticks together to gain an even greater advantage – a self-stick selfie stick. Alex was straight to the point.

'How have we normalised fuckwittery?' she said.

She was bang on. The aerial shot we had of the square was a sad testament to a changing human race. On first glance, no harm. Just people enjoying themselves. But scratch a little deeper and there's a confused picture. The unquenchable desire for self-endorsement via a database of a gazillion photos is now the litmus test of how life is going. Once upon a time, taking a picture of yourself might have been something you had to do quietly, snuck it in while no one was looking. Today it's as normal as breathing, and if you can achieve that by attaching your mobile phone to a five-foot stick, all the better.

Modern innovation knows no bounds and the world of gadgets is always on the lookout for the next gizmo. It can only be a matter of time before the market brings us the next big thing in the 'How to make it even easier to take even more photos of your own face' department. Stand by for the selfie hat (the Samsung sombrero is to die for), selfie shoes (just stare down and click, kids) and, for the sexting generation, selfie pants. They can only be months away. You read it here first.

44.

TRAVIS KALANICK

Travis is the CEO and founder of Uber.

For the unaware, Uber is a global 'cab' company that works via a phone app. There's no number to call or shabby waiting room to sit in, just the click of an app and a cab arrives at your feet. Under Travis's diligent watch, they now operate in almost 500 cities in seventy-six countries. It's a massive operation and the last time I looked the empire was valued at over $65 billion.

Calling Uber a cab company is tricky. They don't self-identify as a cab outfit and get a bit twitchy when referred to as such. Uber is, in fact, a tech company, technically. Their technology merely facilitates a transaction between the two parties: the driver and the rider. Once you're in the cab, Uber's job is done and they simply stand back and trouser 25 per cent of the driver's money. Nice work if you can get it. But they are definitely *not* a cab company, despite hiring over ten thousand cab drivers.

Since Uber landed in London a couple of years ago, there's been a battle. TfL – the world's most useless transport organisation and the body responsible for administering private hire vehicles – has been handing out licences like confetti. There are now almost 120,000 in London alone. The upshot is that the market is diluted, quality reduced and the black cab industry – the worldwide benchmark for taxi excellence – has been fighting for its life. And this isn't just about numbers (the black cab trade can handle competition). There's a whole array of legal ramifications and disputes about how Uber functions and whether its working model falls within the TfL rulebook. As it stands, the law is apparently on Uber's side and the courts seem satisfied that there's nothing to see here, guv. The debate rumbles on.

But there's something else.

Despite Uber's telephone number-like valuation, a boardroom crammed with six-figure-salaried suits (and Travis himself with a personal fortune of over 6 billion quid), the company in the UK pays hardly any tax at all. In 2014, they paid just £22k. That's more or less the collective tax liability of three or four black-cab drivers. The moment Uber reached those giddy heights of being officially labelled rich bastards, they were able to employ the well-known corporate technique of running like a gazelle when the tax man pitches up. Of course, they are doing nothing wrong and, like many similar conglomerates, legally fulfil *all* of their tax-based obligations. But in the case of Uber, the picture is a tad more galling.

I spoke to forty Uber drivers about their own financial situations. Each driver told the same grim story. Because of the overheads, the commission to Uber and TfL's unstoppable penchant for flooding the market with vehicles, they simply don't earn enough money to pay income tax (one paid £300 last year). Unless they are prepared to do an eighty-hour week, it's impossible to make enough money to tip them over the tax-paying threshold. As a result, their life is subsidised with various tax credits from the government.

This all amounts to the utterly bizarre situation where the only people contributing to this equation in terms of tax are you and me in the form of welfare assistance for skint drivers. The upshot here is that the British taxpayer is being used to prop up the existence of one of the world's richest companies. I tend not to subscribe to conspiracy theories, but doesn't all of this begin to resemble a bit of a scandal?

I'm pretty sure Uber would crunch the numbers in a very different way and point out that my survey of forty drivers is hardly scientific. I'm sure their PR department would muster up the Uber Cabbie of the Year, a man who earns a six-figure salary and drives a gold-plated Prius while simultaneously juggling a European property portfolio. They would show me graphs pointing north and spreadsheets outlining the long-term benefits to the UK economy – 'look how many jobs we have created', they would shout in rehearsed unison before forcing a smile and sending me out the door with a flea in my ear. The fact that their long-term business model clearly aims to do away with the human element altogether in the form of driverless cars is not really up for discussion.

Taking an Uber cab *is* cheaper – that's its only selling point. But as this colossal organisation becomes even bigger, those fares will rise. They already use a 'surge price' mechanism, meaning that at busy times, the cost of your trip can increase four-fold. This means that using an Uber goes from being the cheapest in town to the most expensive – top dollar for the bargain basement option. I've no doubt that within a few years they will dominate further and London's finest – the black cab trade – will, just like red phone boxes, become little more than visual trimming for tourists.

I'm confident that Travis Kalanick is an entrepreneurial genius. After all, he has managed to turn shit into actual money. I'm also sure he's a nice bloke. But when it comes to public transportation, the man is a menace. Whatever success his model has had elsewhere, it doesn't fit within the UK and their presence here is as welcome as measles. If you don't give a toss about a low-wage economy and a billion-dollar company paying virtually no tax then go on using them all you like. Just don't purport to care about such things and then jump into a Prius of an evening because you save £3 on your journey.

45.

UBER DRIVERS

If you're thinking of using Uber, you might want to check out their terms and conditions.

> You understand that by using the application and service, you may be exposed to transportation that is potentially dangerous, offensive, harmful to minors, unsafe or otherwise objectionable. You use this application and service at your own risk.

Stone the crows. Can you think of any other product or service that you would happily use having been forewarned by the very people supplying it that you or even your child could be harmed while using it?

> Why not try one of our new range of comfy sofas? They come in a choice of colours and are supplied in either two-seater versions or three. We should warn our customers that in the event that you decide to actually sit on one, a massive spike might – but not necessarily will – fire from the sofa base and disembowel you in the process.

You'd probably opt to steer clear.

Over the past couple of years I have hosted numerous radio debates on the issue of Uber and their presence in the London cab market. I've interviewed the head honchos from TfL, the reps and drivers from the black cab trade and numerous Uber drivers themselves. Uber, the company, have always refused to talk to me. The invitation is still there.

What has become increasingly clear during these debates is that London (and many other cities around the UK – remember, Uber is now very much a national affair) is heading for a New York-type taxi trade where cheap imported labour will be used to create a whole new market in the capital's cab trade. A market which will not merely co-exist with the current one but which will dominate and potentially obliterate it.

Something doesn't sit right here. To become a black-cab driver, you essentially need to give up life for half a decade. There's four years' worth of training in The Knowledge, tens of thousands of pounds in costs and commitment, and enough blood, sweat and tears to make a brace of Olympians stop in their tracks. How could all of *that* suddenly be replaced by a gig that requires absolutely none of these things bar the ownership of a motor?

This chronic redefining of what it takes to be a professional driver in one of the busiest cities on the planet is not just laughable, it's completely idiotic. We're not talking about a village cabbie who ferries old ladies home from church on a Sunday; this is the damn metropolis and there's an entire skill set involved in doing the job properly. No matter how good your TomTom might be, it's never going to replace the knowledge, confidence, safety and instincts of a professional black-cab driver.

Since Uber began their ambitious endeavours in the UK, I had taken a decision never to use them. I had gone all militant on the issue and decreed that I would never set foot in one of their stupid cars. These were the scabs of the roads who were helping to reduce and eradicate the cultural icon that is the black cab. I had become the Arthur Scargill of the piece, making my position clear to both friends and listeners to my radio programme. As far I was concerned, Uber was dead.

My mate Mike had offered up some reasonable journalistic advice. If I was serious about these anti-Uber pontifications then I needed to prove my point more authentically – I needed to use the service. Only then could I confidently bang on about the shortcomings of the world's worst car service.

'Give it a go, you might like it,' Mike said, like a man coaxing his wife into the dark world of extreme bondage.

'I can't do it. It's like asking an arachnophobe to sit in a bath of spiders.'

'You can do it. Just take some deep breaths, register online and give it a go. If it's really that bad, you can then tell all of your listeners what a heap of shit they are. Job done.'

On 1 November 2016, I became an Uber customer. For the next four weeks they would become my default cab service. After that, the app would be deleted and never used again. I would then shower for a week and cleanse myself of my wicked misdemeanour.

If you were applying for a job as a cab driver in a city you didn't know, and in a country you hadn't even lived in for very long, you might imagine that one of your first moves would be to familiarise yourself with some basic landmarks. Fair enough, you're not an expert like the black cabbies, but a good starting point would be to at least get to know some fundamentals. If you were cabbying in Glasgow, it would clearly be sensible to know where George

Square is; in Manchester, you'd be wise to have an idea about how to get to Old Trafford. And in London, it would be seen as best practice to know what Nelson's Column looked like. And where it was. These are pretty key requirements from day one. You would think.

I took a total of nineteen journeys in my four-week trial. Some were short runs around town; most were longer, going from places like Leicester Square in the middle of the capital to Bromley, a borough in the southernmost part of London (or north Kent for the precious). Aside from my very first attempt at using them, when the driver told me he was unable to pick me up because he was travelling north on Charing Cross Road and didn't know how to turn around (the upshot was that he told me to go and have sex with myself), all of the drivers I encountered were supremely polite and smiled lots. Admittedly, it was often a gritted-teeth kind of smile – one that says 'Please don't make this overly complicated because I haven't got a chuffing clue what I'm doing' – but smile they did.

There was also a language barrier. Many of these guys were fairly new to the UK and struggled in broken English. On a couple of occasions we were unable to exchange words at all. This is not only a tad ridiculous in a public-facing job, but it also flags up the issue of basic safety. When you book a cab, you're also buying into a service that you hope can keep you nice and secure – the inability to communicate with the driver clearly compromises that. In terms of their ability behind the wheel, it's hard to know where to begin. I knew these guys were never going to be the best, but nothing could have prepared me for the utter heart-stopping chaos that I was about to endure.

Imagine being dropped in the middle of Moscow or Beirut and told to become a cab driver for the day. Even with the aid of the world's most sophisticated sat-nav equipment, you would, to coin a phrase, be bricking it. Yet this is essentially what you get when you book one of these guys. It was like driving with the world's worst learner driver. The lack of confidence and instinct was palpable. The sense of security non-existent. Despite their best intentions these bozos were utterly clueless. You'd feel more secure if they lobbed a cocker spaniel into the driver's seat.

It's 1.45 in the morning. We're on the M25. Something isn't right. I look up from my phone. The driver is gripping the steering wheel like it was a pair of lapels. His nose is almost glued to the windscreen. He's a man on a mission. I notice the speedo. We're doing 38mph. And we're in the middle lane. Thirty-eight miles per hour on one of the world's biggest and busiest motorways. The late hour means bugger all to the M25 – it's the road that never sleeps. We have sixty-ton juggernauts undertaking us and cars flashing their headlights overtaking. This bozo is either blissfully unaware or scared rigid.

'Mate, you're doing thirty-eight miles an hour – you do know the limit is seventy?'

'Best to be safe,' says the man at the wheel. He clenches a smile into the rear-view mirror, clearly not believing a word of what he has just said.

Best to be safe? Is this bloke for real? He's on a damn kamikaze mission here and he's talking safety. This isn't good.

'Might be best to get into the inside lane,' I suggest, as a three-trailered Post Office truck scoops past, almost peeling off the entire nearside wing of his car. I hear the honk of a horn.

'We come off in one mile. I can move over then,' he says, nodding like a Churchill dog. WTF – am I on some kind of ITV2 hidden camera show? Is Stephen Mulhern about to pop out of the glove compartment and reveal the wacky charade? I try to point out that driving this slowly really isn't a good idea and even more lethal when straddling the middle lane. He tells me that it is the fault of impatient lorry drivers who think they own the road. This man has clearly never driven on a motorway in his life. When we finally reach home, he politely thanks me before asking if I know another route back that avoids the M25 and any other motorways. What kind of professional driver would ask that question to a customer? I ask him if he has ever driven on a motorway before. He giggles nervously before wiping away a bead of sweat from his brow. No, he says. Never.

Two days later. Same motorway, different driver. Again, middle lane all the way, though this time we are cruising at a more reasonable 50mph. But all is not good Chez Prius. I'm suddenly aware that we are no longer in the middle lane. Or any lane. We're on the hard shoulder. Our trusty Uber man is *actually* driving on the hard shoulder.

'Why are we driving on the hard shoulder?' I ask, nervously.

'This is the slip lane,' he says. 'We come off here.'

'No, the slip lane is two miles away. This is the hard shoulder.'

'Slip lane – all OK.'

'No, this is the hard shoulder, mate. We shouldn't be driving here.'

'Slip lane,' he repeats, like Citizen Kane choking out the word Rosebud. 'Don't worry, we come off in a minute,' he adds.

'No, we come off in two miles – this is the hard shoulder.'

'But it leads to the slip lane.'

Shit.

The next day, same motorway, different driver. We were doing a steady 50mph, only this time the driver had selected the outside lane as his preferred space. Sod all the others drivers, this bloke was in his comfort zone and he wasn't budging. I was ensconced on the back seat following a dramatic courtroom battle scene of *Making A Murderer* on my phone. Things were not looking good for Brendan. I was pondering this injustice when the elements hit. And I mean the elements. Out of nowhere, I was blasted with a gust of freezing wind. It came from all directions, knocking me clean from my concentration. I looked up with some urgency only to be hit with another ferocious wave of hard, cold air. I could feel the droplets of winter drizzle hit my face. What the hell was happening? Had this man just lost his windscreen? The reality wasn't far off.

'Why have you just opened your windows?' I enquired through the wind tunnel. I shouted to be heard.

'No problem,' he replied.

No problem? Is this jackass for real? I leant my head between the two front seats, trying to duck the crossfire of freezing air.

'Why are your windows open? It's about two degrees out there.'

'It's important to stay awake,' he shouted back. He nodded at the brilliance of his own health and safety advice. Well, yes, I guess he's kind of right. It is rather important to remain in a non-sleeping state while driving a car on a motorway. Technically he *was* correct.

'Mate, you need to do your windows up, this is a bit silly. And very cold.'

He pondered the question. I saw his hand hover over the window button. Come on buddy, you can do it. Slide those bad boys up. He relented. Sort of. The passenger window slid up, the driver's one remained down.

As the meteorological bombardment continued, the driver attempted to placate me and insisted that this was a very normal thing to do on a night-time journey. He reiterated his need to be kept awake at the wheel. He seemed to think that not only should I understand this, but I was a bit daft not to have worked it out for myself in the first place.

As we reached my house, I asked what was now becoming a standard question. I got the same reply – he had also never driven on a UK motorway in his life. He was also at pains to point out that they are quite unnecessary and inconvenient things that are best avoided. Amazing. I left the car looking a bit like Jim Carrey in that moped scene from *Dumb and Dumber*.

Over my one-month trial I discovered that this service was, to coin a phrase, a bit shit. I am really struggling to believe that the head honchos who run Uber could seriously be satisfied with this level of service themselves and whether they would be happy and relaxed to see their own kids using it.

I totally get the notion of emerging markets and competition, and if this was the story of a small minicab company working out the back of a mate's garage offering cheap local trips in order for punters to save a few quid, I could see where the model was going. But this is the world's biggest provider of cab-based transportation. They are fast becoming the default brand in the UK's capital and beyond. That should worry anyone.

If Uber want to be really honest with their customers, then the least they could do would be to add an amendment to those terms and conditions:

Customers should also be aware that it's completely possible that your driver won't have a fricking clue where they are going. You may also wish to make a will before travelling – this could very well be your last trip, anywhere.

46.

EVAN WRIGHT

I only met Evan because I ended up on the wrong website. It's easily done. I'd been reading the news – the MailOnline side bar, probably – and noticed at the bottom a series of those clickbait stories: 'Ten worst examples of celebrity plastic surgery', 'The ugliest dogs in the world', 'Ten near-death sporting fails'. Each story is accompanied by a little square photo. It's too tempting. Who doesn't want to see a picture of Mickey Rourke and his newly elasticated ears or a spaniel that looks like Donald Trump? I clicked. And that's where the fun began.

There was indeed a worrying photo of some poor mutt that clearly wasn't about to win Crufts. A small caption told me there were twenty more of these beasts ready and waiting. But how do I get to the next photo? There are a dozen arrows and click points on the page. Which one is for me? The page is a mess, with multiple ads for insurance, health products and all manner of financial services. Which arrow am I meant to click?

This, of course, is the whole point. You're *meant* to click the wrong thing. The idea being that some moronic sales agency can go back to their client and tell them that a hundred thousand people clicked on their ad for car insurance. The fact that they were actually trying to find photos of ugly dogs doesn't need to be mentioned. Monetising the internet is still very much at first base, and while second-rate entrepreneurs think that *pages visited* actually equates to anything of value, it's not about to get much further.

I hovered my mouse over one of the arrows and took a punt. And got the wrong page. And thank God I did, because this is how I met Evan.

The page was impressive. There was a ready-to-play video at the top and a big photo of Evan in the middle. There was a quote next to his picture: 'I didn't graduate from college and I'm not a mathematician. I found a way to make a million. It's easy to do and anyone, regardless of experience, can be making money in the next half-hour. Anyone can do it. Now is the time.'

Now is the time?

The video began with a bunch of ordinary people explaining how they had made a fortune within weeks. There were impressive screenshots showing the actual amount they had bagged in less than a month. These were incredible figures. After the testimonials were done, along comes Evan. Sort of. We don't actually see him, but he narrates us through the mechanics of his idea. The video throws up some helpful captions reflecting his words. And what he has to say is mind-blowing.

I want you to make hundreds of thousands of pounds in the next thirty days. I'll even help you do it. I'm going to take you by the hand and guide you to hundreds of thousands of pounds within the next month. If you don't make it, I'll give you £10,000 in cold, hard cash right out of my own pocket. That's right, I guarantee you'll make hundreds of thousands of pounds in the next thirty days or I will give you £10,000 cash. Just for landing on this page you have already made at least £10,000, guaranteed.

But listen, those people you saw at the start of this video all accepted my offer just a few months ago, but I didn't have to give a single one of them £10,000. That's because they all made several *hundred* thousand pounds in the first month. They continue to make money like that every month. So the chances are you're not going to get ten thousand pounds out of me because you will already be making so much more. Hundreds of thousands of pounds in the next thirty days. In a month's time you could be one of these people on the members-only page showing off your six- or seven-figure bank account.

We're not here to sell stuff, nor are we sleazy internet marketing gurus trying to get your credit card number so that we can rip you off.

So put your wallet away and listen closely. Over the next couple of minutes I will explain how you too can get free access to this challenge and be making hundreds of thousands of pounds by this time next month.

Putting aside his slightly dicey use of the English language, Evan Wright is clearly a very nice man. He wants to give me ten grand. In fact, he *will* give me ten grand. If I don't make a million, the lovely Evan will personally deposit £10,000 into my bank account. People often say that human decency is no more, consigned to a distant past. Evan is proof that there are exceptions. He's a beacon of hope and a fine example of how good people will eventually triumph. What a thoroughly fabulous bloke he is. I wish he was my brother.

My instinct was to call my new friend and talk the deal through. If we were to be business partners then a proper chat was needed. Unfortunately, there was no phone number on the website. Maybe I could email him, but it appeared there was no direct way to do this either. On top of all of this, there was another question rattling around in my head. I had been resisting giving it too much thought. I didn't want to think badly of Evan. But what if – and I know this is a shamefully sceptical way of thinking – what if (hypothetically) this whole thing was bollocks?

And so it came to pass that this whole thing *was* bollocks. Of course it was. Evan doesn't actually exist. A quick trip around the interweb will show that the very same claim (and identical webpage) is made by Jason Taylor, Jamie Mason and a litany of others. They are no more real than the apocryphal Nigerian prince who wants to stick 10 million quid into your bank account. In this case, you sign up for the software, stick a chosen amount of money into your newly created account and someone on the other side of the world sticks their virtual hand in and nicks it. I've tried to find out who all the actors are in the video (they are all Brits) and who exactly the photo claiming to be Evan is. No success on that one so far but I'll keep looking.

Internet cons have been with us since Tim Berners-Lee first plugged in his laptop. Most of us spot them a mile off. We also tend laugh like drains when we realise that a stupid person could have fallen for such a blatant ruse. What kind of cretin sticks thousands of pounds into someone else's bank account? But people do and these shysters know full well that for every million people who ignore an obvious con, only one person needs to be taken in. And robbed.

So let's not go down that path of romanticising the crime in that Great Train Robbery/Kray Twins-type way ('They only harmed their own...!' / 'Salt of the earth...') and creating a grudging respect for the genius of the scam. These are thieves in a virtual world, up there with those who show up at a pensioner's house to read the gas meter, only to rob them of their entire life savings. Where is Matt Allwright when you need him?

If anyone knows Evan – www.secrettrick.net – do let me know. However, if you happen to bump into the man in the photo, please don't berate him or start going testicle bound with your size 9s. He's likely to be some poor actor who thought he was posing for a haemorrhoid cream commercial. Will the real Evan Wright please step forward?

47.

GREG WALLACE

Who the hell is Greg Wallace?

When I say, 'Who is Greg Wallace?', what I actually mean is: 'Why does Greg Wallace exist?' As in, where did he come from? He seems to have been around for yonks, yakking away on the box, so I wanted to know what the deal was. How did he arrive in TV land? Did he train as a chef with the Prue Leith School of Food and Wine? Did he cut his teeth in busy Parisian kitchens before making his way back to the UK to set up a chain of restaurants, only to be spotted by a dining TV exec who was intoxicated by the combination of his tasty grub and mardy manner? Something about this man didn't sit right with me; I needed to know what his background was. I was in for a shock. Despite his entire TV persona suggesting otherwise, it turns out that Greg Wallace isn't a chef at all. He's a greengrocer. He flogged carrots for a living.

You might be thinking that you already knew this. But how many people who stumble across one of the UK's top TV food gurus and front man of countless chef-based programmes realise that he isn't actually a chef? There was only one way to answer this. Get onto Twitter. I stuck a photo of Greg onto my feed and asked my followers what they thought he did for a living. Twitter is a curious beast when it comes to questions like this. It was an open goal for any bored commuter or student who fancied themselves as a writer of comedy one-liners. Aside from three people who said they thought he was indeed a chef, every other answer was not publishable without ending up in the High Court.

This was bugging me. I knew it was irrational but I couldn't square the circle. How is a man who stands in judgement and critiques wannabe (and even pro) chefs on their ability to cook not actually a chef himself? *Masterchef* is a global brand. It's sold around the world to millions, so you might think that the mouthy host who takes great pleasure in telling nervous contestants that their ratatouille is a bit manky and their fritters are on the wane might be rolling around in cooking qualifications (as distinct from someone who spent half their life shouting 'Three for a pound' in a Covent Garden market). Was I being conned here? Was I alone in thinking for years that the number one food face on my telly might just have an inner knowledge about cooking the stuff? I needed to know how many others had fallen for this ruse.

My partner suggested – facetiously – that if it bugged me that much, I should do a proper survey. This was getting out of hand, but Greg was now playing with my head.

The challenge was set. The people of Bromley were about to be part of one of the most extensive surveys into Greg Wallace that has ever been carried out. Forget chuggers and those folk who want to sell you God, I was going to take to the streets with a different kind of purpose. Armed with nothing more than a clipboard and big photo of Greg. I had one question: what does this man do for a living?

I took prime position outside M&S. It's a tricky thorough-fare in Bromley High Street. There was a man from Amnesty and a girl trying to get people to sign away their dosh for sick cats. They obviously wondered who this new kid on the block was. Maybe I should have had one of those massive oversized charity jackets with an embroidered image of Greg's face on the back to authenticate my status.

'Excuse me, do you know who this is?'

The man nodded.

'Yeah, it's Greg Wallace,' he replied.

'What does he do for a living?'

'He's a chef.'

One out of one. Bingo.

'Excuse me, do you know who this is?' This time it was an elderly lady.

'Is it Norris from Coronation Street?' The woman looked back for confirmation.

'No. Think food,' I said.

'Oh yes, it's that Greg fellow from the cookery programme.'

'What does he do for a living?'

'Well, he's a chef, isn't he?' said the woman rhetorically.

Two out of two. It's looking good.

I spent a gruelling eight minutes carrying out my street survey. And person after person confirmed my suspicions. The entire world thinks that Greg Wallace is a chef. Why wouldn't they? In the past few years he's not only presented numerous versions of *Masterchef* but also *Saturday Kitchen*, *What's Really In Our Food?*, *Ready Steady Eat*, *Sunday Brunch*, *What's Cooking*, *Daily Brunch* and *The Junk Food Challenge*. All programmes you might reasonably associate with someone who cooks for a living.

I appreciate that the world of TV is a bit potty when it comes to who fronts up our daily diet of onscreen delights (more on this in a moment), but this Greg lark was beginning to look insane. I asked a mate who works in a fairly senior position at the BBC. She had clearly developed a case of Stockholm Syndrome.

'But you have to understand, Greg is all about the food. He lives and breathes food. He's been around food all his life.' She seemed completely unconvinced by her own argument. Following her logic, my Aunty Pat, who has worked in Tesco for twenty-eight years, would be equally qualified to be a *Masterchef* host.

But it gets worse. In recent times, Mr Wallace has diversified and moved on to more worthy matters. Not only does he retain that peak-time gig as a non-chef on a chef programme, but our spud-headed spud vendor is now dispensing nutritional advice for hard-up families who need to eat well for less. In fact, the programme is ingeniously called *Eat Well for Less*. Turns out that Greg's other area of non-expertise is in the world of culinary economics. What he doesn't know about a cheeky knocked-down bag of Wehani rice isn't worth knowing, they say.

It can only be a matter of time before this whole thing gets out of hand. Where could he be let loose next? *Wallace Does Heart Surgery*, maybe, with Greg getting down and deep into the clogged-up valves of a gluttonous nation? I asked my BBC mate what she thought of the idea. She smirked, returning my sarcasm. But somewhere in there I fear she banked the idea, savouring the proposal for the next commissioning meeting, maybe. Keep your eye on the schedules, kids.

48.

MISCAST TV PRESENTERS

To be fair, Greg is not alone in being lobbed in front of a camera with a tenuous link to the subject matter. It's an issue that sits buried within a decades-old media mystery, a conundrum that no one has ever got to the bottom of: who commissions the commissioners? Just who are the secretive cartel of faceless execs who decide what we watch on the telly? And what *is* the criterion – the litmus test – of what is sure to be a big hitter? No one, it seems, is privy to the secret code that unlocks the magic formula that brings comedy, drama and documentaries to a grateful nation. But what we *do* know is that quite a lot of weird shit seems to end up on our TVs.

Top of the list of unfathomables is the curious penchant of hiring actors and comedians to front documentaries. I'm unsure if this is meant to a be quick and easy ratings fix by getting folk watching stuff that ordinarily they would swerve like a mad thing or a genuine attempt to re-educate the nation via the more accessible conduit of celebrity. Either way, and in a chronic subverting of the definition of 'documentary', we now have a stunning array of TV's finest bringing us a genre of telly once delivered only by the likes of Herzog and Theroux. The roll-call is quite something.

I guess Ross Kemp was an early contender on this one. The former hard man of soapland is now the default booking for anything related to war and hassle. He's the front man who knows no fear, and when it comes to getting down and dirty with our boys on the front line, it's Kemp who treads where few others would dare. In fact, I tend not to take any news of an impending international war too seriously these days unless I think Ross is about to pitch up and get stuck in too. How we've marvelled at his SAS pursuits, his precarious trips to Iraq and Afghanistan and those risky brushes with toothless Brazilian gang members. Make no mistake, when it comes to a scuffle, there's no one else who can truly tell it like it is. At one point I was so utterly enamoured by Ross and his military endeavours that I almost wanted to apply, train and sign up and actually become an *EastEnders* actor myself. It never happened. Stephen Fry also plays a lead role here, with a plethora of documentaries on everything from snooker to brown bears. Then there's Joanna Lumley on the Northern Lights, Keith Allen investigating Tourette's syndrome, Sue Perkins on the Mekong River, Rory McGrath in a boat, Ewan McGregor on a bike, this bat-shit crazy list is never-ending.

And then someone in TV land decided it was really time to take the piss. The BBC wanted to make a documentary on immigration. They were going to explore the *real* story, not the sanitised version peddled out by mischievous tabloids. They were going for the qualified view, they wanted *in depth* – a programme that gave this divisive issue the true gravitas it deserved. But who would you get to present such a programme?

Trevor McDonald maybe – a man who could combine his journalistic skills with his own immigrant backstory? Michael Portillo, a former minister, son of immigrants and now a fairly serious face in television presentation? Or maybe they could drag Boutros Boutros-Ghali back into the fold; his CV would surely be a bit of a clincher. Sadly, none of these got the gig. Instead the job of fronting the BBC's biggest documentary on immigration in recent years went to… Nick and Margaret, that pair that used to be on *The Apprentice*. Buggeration.

What the hell went on in that commissioners meeting? By what process did they arrive here? Was there a group discussion and a heated stand-off? Did they have an *X Factor*-style deck of cards showing all the potential names and faces until someone eventually cut through the impenetrable silence with the immortal words: 'If we're going to do this properly, we need Nick and Margaret'? I would seriously pay serious money to get a serious answer as to why someone thought this was a good idea.

Of course, we'll never know. The commissioning code can't be broken, and until the next almighty howler (*Mary Berry does Sumo*, maybe) poor old Nick and Mags are left looking a bit daft, all because some doofus at Telly Towers simply liked the idea of using them.

Most of this nonsense comes under the predictable banner of TV wanting to be all things to all people – a delusive and, ultimately, wholly unachievable objective. It's a common theme: from the token comedian on the *Question Time* panel through to the Prime Minister popping up on *Loose Women*, the world of telly loves nothing more than a bit of cool mix and match.

And then there's the biggest offender of them all. A man who should know better…

49.

ANDREW MARR

I like Andrew Marr. His almost sacred presence in the tricky world of political journalism is not in question. He has more than carved out his rightful place as one of the nation's leading faces of current affairs. He's also someone who made his way to the very top through undiluted graft rather than via the passport of his mum and dad's contacts book. All impressive stuff. But something has gone badly wrong. And it's all the fault of the very programme that bears the mighty one's name. *The Andrew Marr Show* has some explaining to do.

For starters, who in the name of Lord Reith's pants made those opening titles? Marr is a serious journalist, not a Belgian detective. Yet, for some inexplicable reason, the head honchos at BBC HQ have taken the most studious-looking bloke on the box and tried to morph him into some kind of curious roving enigma. The chosen method for achieving this impossible feat was to lob him into a pale-grey Nissan Figaro, chuck in an Agatha Christie-esque theme tune, and then film his tenacious journey through the streets of London Town. Presumably with the aim of inviting the viewers to join in a kind of collective 'Look, everybody, here comes Andy' type frenzy (as distinct from the desire to eat your own face). This embarrassing spectacle was only superseded when they ditched the micro-car and replaced it with a customised green Vespa scooter.

This is just the start of the grim journey.

In its drive to camouflage the entire political nature of its own show (and presumably to woo hungover students into thinking that there's more to Sunday morning politics than unrecognisable opposition MPs banging on about the toxic Tories), Team Marr do what all good TV programmes think they have to do. Introduce some showbiz.

> In a moment we'll be getting into the heart of the Middle East debate and attempting to dissect the latest developments coming out of the West Bank. We'll also bring you the latest on exactly what President Trump intends to do next over that controversial travel ban. But first, here's Carey Mulligan...

What the...? How did this happen? This show is meant to be the backbone of all things current affairs-related – the oracle of the BBCs political output. This is my Sunday morning appointment to see our Westminster masters held to account by the mighty Andrew and his big forensic brain. Yet week after God-darn week, I'm offered all manner of global stars peddling their latest wares. Bill Nighy, Elton John, Martin Freeman (twice in a year), Kate Winslet and Robert Redford are a mere handful of names who have got up close and personal on Andy's big sofa of celebrity joy. He's got a bigger guest list than *The Graham Norton Show*.

Eventually, the UK's number one current affairs show returns to that delicate issue of, er, current affairs. The Chancellor, the

PM and even the occasional President may well join Andrew for that final political tête-à-tête. Thank the Lord. But as Mr M wraps up the show, there's one further treat in store for us all. Some music. What else?

It's clearly a well-established staple of the Marr format that a good politics show should always end with a nice song. Chrissie Hynde, Sinead O'Connor and Keane have all knocked out that final number in the name of cool TV. Once in a while – and in a fragile attempt not to be rumbled as being too celeb-obsessed – they decide to go for a more cultural vibe. As Andy smiles and waves goodbye, up pops a chronically out-of-place ensemble of South American musicians playing local music from the Chilean streets of Puerto Chacabuco. You can almost see the entire viewing audience dribbling into their brioche. This insane farce is then matched, cringe for cringe, by the fact that whichever poor politico happens to be the last guest on the show has to remain glued to the sofa while the rhythmic finale plays out. The bilious upshot of this means we are forced to witness the likes of Philip Hammond getting all cool and funky as he foot-taps along to some smooth Latin riffs. This is a full two minutes and nine seconds of my life that I can never get back.

50.

THE ELDERLY PERSON IN SMALL CAR CLUB

The man in front was already driving at an ever-so-slightly annoying 25mph. We were in a 30 zone. This old duffer was having none of it. Best to be safe. I could see the big yellow speed camera half a mile ahead. It had been planted on the right-hand side of the road like a huge metal giraffe, now as common a sight on UK roads as traffic lights. Hardly a motorist in the land hasn't been collared at least once by the lightning flash; a one-second spark, three points on your licence and a hundred quid slides from your bank account courtesy of the Digital Police.

The man in front was clearly having this exact thought. Best to be safe. We were twenty metres away when the brakes were applied. When I say applied, I don't mean gently pressed in order to slow down in an appropriate manner. This man hit the anchors as if a small child had just walked out in front of him. An instant screech cut through the midday air like a blade. The inevitable nauseous smell of burning rubber soon followed. I braked too. As did the man behind. The driver, now almost stationary, took a brief visual recce before continuing his journey, gradually rebuilding his speed back to the default 25mph.

The problem is two-fold. Firstly, why the hell was he braking anyway? He was doing 25. He didn't need to slow down, he was already well within the speed limit. But perhaps more baffling, it wasn't *his* speed camera. The camera was for drivers on the *other* side of the road: it was trying to nab motorists going the other way. Yet the mere fact that he had seen the damn thing was enough to panic him into taking totally unnecessary action. He seemed blissfully unaware of the debacle. As we pulled up to the next junction, I pulled alongside. I wanted to get a glimpse of the world's most paranoid driver. And there he was in all his minuscule glory. About a hundred years' worth of man. Boris Karloff in a 306.

The Elderly Person in a Small Car Club have been causing mayhem on our roads since Karl Benz put away his spanners. But they have been afforded a curious protection under the wonky umbrella that generalising is now a crime akin to second-degree murder. You can't tar everyone with the same bad brush, and all that. We're also regularly offered the frankly bullshit 'fact' that our elders are statistically the safest drivers on the road – they have fewer accidents. You can't seem to convince insurance companies that being *overcautious* is just as dangerous as not giving a toss. If you feed all the data into a computer, there is nothing in the algorithm that throws up paranoid idiocy as a reason to penalise a driver in the premium department. It simply says that Mr Karloff is less likely to have a prang. Nothing about him being 5,000 times more likely to cause one. In the fuzzy world of insurance, Boris is the safer bet. The fact that he's merrily driven off up the road oblivious to the carnage he's left behind him counts for diddly.

None of this should be controversial. It's a cast-iron fact that as we get older, things slow down. Our reactions and instincts are not the same as they once were. Our capacity to make instant decisions and to calculate risk and error are gradually reduced. This is no more a revelation than saying that an octogenarian probably isn't going to be quite as good as the Brownlee brothers in a triathlon. But for some reason we have been coerced into believing that none of these biological and physical facts should have any bearing on someone getting behind the wheel of a ton of metal. All the unarguable realities of the ageing process are apparently removed the moment you open a car door and jump in.

We can all see evidence to the contrary. How many more times do we have to read about some old codger getting all confused at a roundabout and driving in the wrong direction down a motorway? How often are we going to see delicate old ladies almost have the side of their vehicle shaved off because they thought the middle lane was the safer option? There's a litany of evidence of lovable OAPs getting things terribly wrong on our roads, yet nobody at the DVLA seems particularly bothered.

But there is a solution here. The UK is missing a trick. We are constantly fed stories about the societal and economic perils of an ageing population. People are living longer and this throws up enormous challenges for the powers that be. How will we finance our future generations? How can the pension pot stretch to accommodate lives that are now extended by more than twenty years? The good and the great from No. 10 and the Treasury have been pondering this question for yonks. The answer is staring them in the face.

Let's encourage the nation's old folk to become Uber

drivers. Travis and his empire will surely be only too happy to take them on. Could there be a more logical way to get older people back into the workplace than giving them a gig that require no professional experience and where the ability to cause mayhem is standard practice? A pensioner in a Prius should be commonplace, as common as seeing old folk playing bowls. This would address finance, employment and social interaction all in one swoop. On top of that, as a passenger, you can be regaled with stories about the war, grandchildren and the constant reminder of how old they are, as you enjoy the ride.

51.

CLUELESS PARENTS

At what point, when a kid is behaving like an arse, does a parent make the conscious decision to do absolutely nothing about it?

I was in a Harvester (sometimes there really is no other place) when a blood-curdling squeal sounded from the other side of the restaurant. It was the sound of unquestionable distress. Something unpleasant was going on. For a fleeting moment I wondered if the chef was culling a goat or something. Maybe the Harvester was indulging in some kind of religious slaughter to appease an increasingly diverse clientele (and I thought the salad bar was progressive). There it was again, the same tormented shriek, only louder. All eyes focused on the source.

'You can't have a Happy Meal because this isn't McDonald's. Now eat ya chicken,' the woman shouted directly into the face of the four-year-old kid. She had clearly never seen that Nanny programme on Channel 4. There was a three-second stare-off between mother and child before the kid let out another almighty scream. The piercing wail cut the atmosphere like a hatchet. This time the mother employed a different technique: she ignored it. This had the brilliant effect of prompting the child to simply amp up the decibels, carrying on screaming. The mother carried on ignoring.

The rest of us took the very British approach of optimism over pessimism. As Junior continued to scream like an ignited chimpanzee, fifty-eight fellow diners carried on as if nothing much was happening. The collective – but chronically misplaced – belief being that it'll soon stop, it's bound to. But it didn't stop.

The distressed kid was now convulsing like some kind of crazed child of the corn, rocking backward and forwards in its high chair as the shrills continued. The mum and her mate carried on stuffing their fizzogs with ribs and chops. Sooner or later, the mum is going to get up and take the kid outside, right?

Wrong.

I'd gone through a prawn starter and was halfway through the main course and this howling bairn was showing no signs of giving up. The waiter had made a vain attempt to step in, bringing colouring pencils and paper to the table. The child was having none of it. The mother assured the waiter that all was good, dismissing his claims of a mass disturbance with a giggle. The waiter, who, let's face it, isn't paid to be a proxy parent to wolf-like kidlings, scuttled off as if the mistake was all his.

'He'll be all right in a minute,' said the mum, via a gob full of chips.

In a minute? This had gone on for nearly half an hour. Anything that can scream that loudly needs to be ejected, and fast. But Mum had other ideas. There were calories to be had and no screaming brat was about to stand in the way of that.

As fellow diners muttered and scoffed their way to an accelerated exit, the raucous din simply carried on. The mum had zero intention of doing anything that might just show a scintilla of consideration for anyone else around her. She was oblivious. After all, it's just kids being kids.

This was pretty much the mantra uttered by another contender for the compulsory sterilisation programme. Different scene, same sad deal.

The man seemed more concerned about completing his Facebook post than looking after his own child. Being buried deep in your smartphone is not an unreasonable way to want to spend a Saturday afternoon, unless of course you are the person solely responsible for a six-year-old child as you walk through the pet department of a garden centre.

We were in the fish section. A dozen rows of large tanks housing all manner of breeds and types. The tanks formed the aisles and happy fish fans can gawp their way from one sort to another. Kids love all this nonsense, sticking their faces up to the glass trying to scare the life out of 300 bloodfin tetras. This is where I encountered the child fish-murderer. The commotion began with a very upset man from the pet store.

'Noooooooooo...! What are you doing? Stop him!' The line was delivered in a kind of verbal slow motion. The man bounded from his till over to where the deed had occurred.

'What are you doing, you've killed the fish!' he said, as distraught as you like.

The kid smiled, like Hannibal Lecter Jr.

There was indeed a fish incident. The child had lobbed his toy digger into one of the tanks and collared a fish in the process. The fish didn't look to be in good shape. The kid had scored a direct hit and young Nemo was wiggling away on his side, fighting for his life. Fish have no protocol for when one of their own is involved in a clear hit and run. Their default position is to leg it (or fin it) and pretend nothing much is going on. It was left to the human race to take care of matters. The man from the store grabbed a small net and scooped the poor fish from the tank.

'It's dead. Look what you've done,' he said.

This was a cue for the dad to step in and dispense his own observations.

'It was already like it.' The dad gestured as if he'd just uttered an unarguable truth. The fact that he was nowhere near the tank – or his own fish-killing child – when it happened was a mere irrelevance to Superdad.

'He just threw his toy car into the tank and hit the fish. Your child has killed the fish,' argued the man with the net.

'We don't know that, do we?' said the dad, raising an odd smile, like he was Judge Rinder.

'We kind of do,' replied the man, reasonably. 'Look, it's not even wiggling now.'

'I take it you don't have kids?' The dad was now on the defensive and had decided to employ the twat card by trying to argue that the man's lack of offspring (which he had no proof of) somehow precluded him from the world of logic and judgement. 'If you did, you would know that kids do silly things sometimes, it's in their nature.'

The dad shook his head, grabbed his son's hand and buggered off.

Fish Boy and the Banshee Child (didn't John Peel used to play their albums...?) are far from isolated cases. This mad proclivity for saying jack shit when your child is palpably doing something wrong or rude appears to be a bit of a thing. The rule of thumb isn't hard to fathom here: if your kid does go off-piste and behaves like a super-charged arse merchant, it is actually your job to bring them back. And 'fess up. No one will think badly of you.

And if your child does happen to murder an animal as they wander innocently through those early years, call in a special-ist. You might have something a tad more worrying than the cost of a new fish going on.

52.

THE PROFESSIONALLY OFFENDED

Where did all offended people go before social media? What did they do with all that fake angst and plastic indignation? Was there a private club somewhere, where delicate offendees could gather to exchange tales of how their lives would never be the same because someone off the telly said something that they had decided to take offence at? Or did they simply keep it all pent up, only to unleash their rage on an unsuspecting partner in years to come?

The vogue of transposing disagreement into offence isn't entirely new. For years there's been a small but perfectly formed contingent of halfwits who have decreed that if they don't like the look or smell of something then neither should anyone else. Ignoring is not an option; offence needs to be taken, and quickly. Additionally, grovelling apologies are required, the offender needs to be named, shamed and hopefully fired and, where possible, criminal proceedings should follow. All based on a different point of view.

Twitter is the great amphitheatre of our times and whatever its many plus points and fascinations, it has also become an echo chamber for silly opinions and wayward ideas – the perfect platform for self-righteous buffoons to get all bothered about stuff that doesn't really matter.

The left-wing Labour MP Jack Dromey found himself on the receiving end of some faux outrage after he posted a photo of himself with a constituent called Pikey. You can see where this is going. Young Pikey is a postman and Jack was on a visit to his local sorting office when the man from the mailroom asked for a photo. The Labour MP dutifully obliged and even put the picture up on his own Twitter feed along with a 'Me and Pikey' caption. It took precisely 1.2 nanoseconds for Jack Dromey's world to temporarily end.

Twitter went into meltdown. There were calls for Jack's incarceration and the constabulary were hastily called in to investigate. One person even wrote a letter to Sir Bernard Hogan-Howe (the UK's most senior police officer), asking for an inquiry. Jack was clearly a mad racist with a pathological hatred of gypsies. Why else would he be putting words like Pikey into a tweet? The evidence was clear: Jack was banged to rights.

Later that day, a crestfallen Jack returned to Twitter to try to clear up the mess by apologising if his tweet had been badly worded. It counted for nothing. Jack was a dead man. Never try to stand in the way of someone who is professionally offended. One keyboard crusader named Hammy was virtually ODing on offence: 'Disgraceful. This is incitement to racial hatred. Pikey is a horrid thing to call anyone. Expect a knock on your door from Plod.'

So not only is he arguing that Jack is a secret racist but that he's actively encouraging others to become race haters too. There's no dilly-dallying in Hammy's world; based on the crimes he's alleging, Jack should be serving at least three years at Her Majesty's pleasure by sundown.

Let's just park up the fact that Jack Dromey is a Labour MP and not a member of the Tea Party movement. His credentials on equality and inclusion are there to find for anyone who cares to look them up. But did anyone seriously think that this was what Jack meant? That a socialist MP had taken to a public forum and was actually using a racial slur to have a pop at a postman? Did these clowns not think that *maybe* something else was going on here, that perhaps it was a play on his name or, as it turned out, his nickname, as in Pike from *Dad's Army*? It was all to no avail. The tweets kept on coming and poor old Jack had no choice to lay low and let the moment pass.

And if you thought it was only in the real world where the offendees found things to offend them, then think again. A while back, TV soap *Coronation Street* got all offensive when it committed the despicable crime of writing some dialogue for a character.

Eva Price is a dizzy but lovable twenty-something in *Corrie*. In the offending scene, she nips into the hairdressers, looks in the mirror and, devastated by the state of her hair, utters the line: 'I've got more roots than Kunta Kinte.' She followed it up with: 'No idea who that is, by the way, just something my mum used to say.'

It was at this point, on a Monday evening at about half seven, that Twitter almost came to a grinding halt. The offendees had been awoken. A new subject had been found. Across the land, like Romero zombies, they dutifully sprang into action, salivating at the task ahead. They could hardly get to their keyboards fast enough. This one had all the ingredients. In terms of being offended, this was bullseye territory.

For those who don't know the story, Kunta Kinte was a character from the novel *Roots: The Saga of an American Family*. The book was adapted into a hit TV miniseries back in the '70s and is based on the story of a young man taken from Gambia and sold as a slave.

The dead wood from the Twittersphere took no time in identifying the offence. Firstly, it was racist – that was a basic, unarguable, cast-iron fact. Secondly, it poked fun at slavery. This was a lethal combination. What's not to be offended about?

The tweets were quite something:

ITV have really done it this time. Since when was it OK to be racist on Corrie?

Racism on Corrie now. Well done ITV. Hang your heads

Hey ITV, would you have written I've got more secrets than Anne Frank's Diary? Thought not. Racial Bias

The last one is a beauty because the comparison doesn't even work. 'I've got more roots than Kunta Kinte' is like saying 'I've got more front than Blackpool'. It's a play on words, a pun. Words which, as the script went on to explain, were actually attributed to her old northern mum from back in the '70s. There's no reference to race or slavery and only someone who is braindead or stupid could have found any offence in the line.

In any case, it's a fricking TV drama. Do we want Scorsese

to moderate his dialogue when talking about the Mob? Should all literature and music be burnt and destroyed based on its often inappropriate use of language or reference points? Again, such logic was totally lost and the social media numbskulls continued with their campaign, clearly hoping for a criminal investigation into Eva Price and her shit hair. There wasn't one.

The offendees' list of outrage is long and laborious. No person or idea is safe from these indignant loons. Over the years they have brought us some beauties: we've had Chris Morris and his brilliant parody on how some aspects of the media deal with the issue of paedophilia, which apparently some people thought was an actual documentary; we've had a camp judge on *The X Factor* making a camp remark about a camp contestant, which received 4,000 complaints (that's not a typo); some mad Christians who wanted to ban a West End musical because they, er, didn't like it (and they didn't ban it either); a chronically stupid student who wanted Oxford University to knock down a statue of Cecil Rhodes because of Rhodes's unsavoury part in history (if you follow that logic, we'd have to knock down Canterbury Cathedral and most of Rome); Transport for London, who upset some hatchet-faced douchebags with some words on a railway notice board that was claimed to be sexist when it definitely wasn't; and, more recently, pretending you're offended because gender signs on public toilets don't take into account the feelings of 'non-binary' people.

Even Stephen Fry, a man who couldn't cause offence if he sniffed cocaine off a Buckingham Palace lavatory seat, found himself on the receiving end of a Twitter bashing after presenting a BAFTA to his friend and jokingly referring to her a being 'dressed as a bag lady'. The offendees were out of the hatches quicker than you could say Milo Yiannopoulos:

> Disgusting words from Stephen Fry. How would you feel if someone said that YOU came dressed as an old queen.

I can confidently say that he wouldn't give a toss.
Fry was quick to tweet back:

> Will all you sanctimonious fuckers fuck the fuck off. Jenny Beavan is a friend and joshing is legitimate. Christ I want to leave the planet

Beautiful.

Taking offence is a choice. You simply can't turn your own personalised idea of what bothers you into a world view. It's yours and yours alone. Trying to mobilise a pretend army via Twitter to join in your crusade doesn't intellectualise or authenticate your opinion. If you don't like something you see, read or hear, keep it to yourself, I guarantee most people won't give a toss.

Social media didn't invent the offendees but it has exacerbated them. They aren't going away any time soon, so watch your back. I learnt a while ago that trying to reason with the chronically offended is a fool's errand. They've made up their minds and the last thing they need is anyone trying to dilute their indignation with rationale and logic.

To make matters so much worse, organisations, terrified of a backlash, have now taken to apologising for their non-offensive behaviour. This has, regrettably, become the default position. TfL apologised despite not being sexist, *The X Factor* did the same despite not being homophobic, Jack Dromey had to say sorry despite not being anti-gypsy and ITV even edited out their non-offensive line from the catch-up episodes of *Corrie*.

How the hell has the human race lost such an immense sense of perspective? Perhaps these paranoid companies need to adopt a bit more growth in the spinal department. Instead of rolling over like demented woodlice, scared witless because some Twitter turkey thinks they're not nice people, how about cut-and-pasting that Stephen Fry tweet and posting it back onto the offendees' walls on an hourly basis. Would that offend them? Probably, but who gives a toss.

53.

MEN'S HAIRDRESSERS

With respect to Sedan, Adam, Mr Ducktail and anyone else who has ever cut my hair, most hairdressers are pretty shit at their job.

For years we have all lived under the assumption that cutting hair is a trade, like being a mechanic or a plumber. It isn't. Anyone can do it. Two weeks with a pair of scissors and a good hairdryer and you'll be as qualified as Vidal Sassoon.

'How do you want it cut?'

'You know how you did it last time? Can you do it like that?'

'Yeah, sure.'

Forty-five minutes later you walk out the place with a haircut that looks nothing like the way they did it last time. That's because your hairdresser has just fobbed you off with a pack of lies. They can't actually remember how they did it last time; they never could. They just made it up. I'm not sure what happens in the world of girls' hair, but for us blokes this is standard stuff. Cutting men's hair is an international con job.

In fairness, it's a big ask. Your hairdresser has probably cut 200 heads of hair since you were last there, so why would they remember how they cut yours? It's a simple answer: they told you they could. They even smiled and imparted a placating look of *don't panic* as they assured you that all would be OK. These are skilled people, remember, the architects of all things hair-related, and part of that skill is their unique ability to recall *exactly* what they did to your high barnet the last time you came in. So they say.

I had initially thought that maybe their total failure to cut hair in the way I had asked was down to distraction. Let's be honest, it takes no time at all for a snipper to drift off on a verbal jolly about their love life, their night on the lash or the problems of Brexit (rarely the last one, but you take the point). I've lost count of how many times I've sat in that chair only for the 'stylist' to suddenly stop, scissors and comb held aloft like a pair of sem-aphore flags, while they bang on about some insane nonsense that's meant to be of interest to me. What's with the pauses in proceedings? Why are you stopping? If you want to talk, then talk and snip. You don't actually have to stop each time you add another layer to a very interesting story about why your other half spends too much time on Facebook. In fact, here's a better idea. Don't tell me the story at all. It says hairdresser's on the sign outside, not hairdresser's and occasional anecdotal parlour.

But it wasn't the distraction issue that was the cause of the problem. It was the simple but scandalous reality that cutting hair just isn't that much of a skill in the first place. When I was a kid, I imagined that this 'profession' was a science meets art-type affair. I had envisaged them spending years fine-tuning the secret trichological code that would eventually allow them the heady status of being an officially qualified person. I now know that this is far from reality.

In order to try to convince gullible punters that there's more to this chopping hair lark than meets the eye, they have come up with an ingenious idea. They have implemented a structured pricing system dependent on who cuts your hair. You now get a choice: you can have a simple 'stylist', a 'senior stylist' or, if you really want to push the boat out and have a proper haircut, a 'style executive'. Who would have thought it – a style *executive*. Flipping heck. What kind of genius came up with that idea? I'm pretty sure that if you took that notional concept into *Dragon's Den*, Peter Jones would be on you like a rash. Here's a business model that is 'fessing up in advance that your haircut could be carried out to one of three different standards? Can you imagine that happening in any other profession?

> And how would you like the chef to cook your food today, sir? You can have it a bit shit and raw by Glenn, or we could bring in Alphonso, who is quite good but still not the best, frankly. Or, if you really want to push the boat out, we can get Bert to cook it properly. He's an executive.

It's a reality which snip-merchants have tried to keep quiet for years: it won't actually matter which choice you make, they will all do the same job. And it won't look anything like the way they did it last time. Unless salons are going to start keeping filing cabinets stuffed with notes and photos of your coiffured noggin, then best they quit the BS. If you go into any big city in the UK now, it won't take long to find a hairdresser's who are asking for £75 for a bloke's haircut. Sod that, get down to a traditional barber's and pay 15 quid. I promise you, it won't be five times inferior to the trim the *executive* thieves are offering.

And if you leave school and can't quite work out what you want to do for a living, why not give hairdressing a go? A few swift sessions in the salon and a couple of goes on an old wig and you'll be let loose on a thousand bonces within no time at all. It's that easy.

54.

SCHNOZ CRIMINALS

Hair is very much on the contemporary menu. Men and women have become more than a little obsessed with trims, skims and waxes. Blokes can go for a back, sack and crack number (where a nice person waxes up your testicles) and women have an almost limitless choice in bikini-line options. On top of that, eyebrows can be raised, widened or even tattooed, and for men, facial hair has made a curious comeback with handle-bar moustaches and Captain Birdseye beards all up for the taking. We've never cared more about hair than we do today. This obsession, however, hasn't reached all parts of the population. Or all parts of the anatomy.

Some things are just plain wrong. You wouldn't walk around in a public place with your underpants hanging around your ankles, showing off your little bits and pieces. This would be seen as not conducive to basic decency. Folk would point and stare and no doubt the local magistrates would eventually have a word. And rightly so. Despite living in an era when freedom of choice and personal expression are sacred, there are still limits. And while making harsh judgements on how other people choose to dress or accessorise is now seen as a crime akin to fascism, surely we can all agree that some things are simply, and unarguably, wrong.

So what the hell is the deal with nose hair? At what point do you look in the mirror and not notice that you have eighteen feet of hair dangling from your hooter? Are you unaware? Do you just not give a toss? Or do you think it breaks some kind of EU law if you try to do something about it? How can you *not* notice?

This problem is primarily, but not exclusively, the domain of men. Old men. That said, I've seen more than of one of these snout crimes perpetrated by the under-forties. My old geography teacher was a case in point. This oddball thought nothing strange about looming over your desk to check your work just inches from your head, giving you a unique glimpse of his unkempt schnoz. It looked like he had a couple of members of ZZ Top in there. How could he *not* know? How would a 35-year-old man wake up in the morning and not at some point realise that the big thing in the middle of his face needed a bit of a trim? This man was married, too, which makes it even more mysterious. Would his wife not have a problem with this? I'm sure she would notice if he decided not to shave for seven weeks, so why the silence on the nostrils? How are these pests so spectacularly oblivious to what is, by anyone's standards, a very unsavoury state of affairs?

I'm amazed that more isn't made of this. Given the never-ending fascination we have with vanity and personal grooming, with TV shows and magazines constantly banging on about the need to look lovely, why isn't this one top of this list? Shouldn't there be public information commercials highlighting the crime, complete with a deep-voiced strapline warning us that nose hair is the enemy of the people?

I regularly spot professional older men, nicely suited and booted in all other respects, but utterly oblivious to their damn nose hair. I appreciate that face-care isn't quite as high on the agenda for these guys as it might be for their younger counterparts, but wouldn't someone around them point them in the direction of a nose trimmer? We simply can't have old codgers mooching around the place looking like the Sasquatch.

And it's not just noses. Ears, too. Once you hit about thirty-five, those things *will* start sprouting. But, for reasons unknown, it would take the threat of a bullet to the head to get them to do something about it. Do these hairy types really think they look OK? Would they honestly not concur that the old King Lears are best seen without an unsavoury mass of fuzz poking out of them? Surely this is a matter of fact, not opinion. Yet, here we are, in the common era, with folk thinking nothing of being seen out in public places with ears that look like they've been stolen from the *Lord of the Rings* costume department.

Once in a while, you spot the ultimate trilogy of face crimes. The ears, nose *and* the eyebrows. Spotting one of these buggers is like getting a Wonka Golden Ticket. They're rare, but they are out there. I'm tempted to think they are mostly eccentric sorts, professors and the like, who would see vanity and grooming as the domain of the imbecile. If you spot one of these bozos, please educate their apparently already educated brains into what passes as facially acceptable.

It goes against my better judgement to call for government intervention, but if this carries on we will have no choice but to insist that our political masters introduce a compulsory trimming programme where we employ feisty men with large nets to take to the streets and capture The Hair People. If Theresa May is looking for volunteers, count me in. I'll be the first in the queue, armed with a pair of industrial tweezers, a Philips Trim Buddy 9000 and a very large bin bag.

55.

PEOPLE WHO DON'T KNOW HOW TO QUEUE

The queue is order out of chaos.
The queue is civility.
The queue is progression.
Anonymous, circa 1900

The woman in the Post Office queue was going tonto. She was having words with the man in front. He'd committed a queue crime and she was, quite rightly, pointing out the error of his ways.

Cashier number ten, please.

Cashier number four, please.

Stunning: two tills available at exactly the same time. It always feels like a massive gain in life when you get two for one like that. But the queue didn't move. For the seventh time, the man in front of the old lady was staying put. He was too busy taking in the surroundings, like he was in a museum.

'Excuse me,' she said. 'Can you just keep moving?'

'We'll all get there eventually,' replied the man, calmly. 'It won't make it go any quicker just because I move a few feet.'

He smiled as if he had the support of the entire world on his side.

He clearly hadn't considered how his wisdom might play out to those at the back of the line. When you're in a very long queue, the only thing you need is progress. It becomes your best friend. You need to know that the thing is moving in the right direction. If Matey in the middle is taking some kind of Buddhist approach to matters, the system crumbles and all hope is dashed. You can't mess with the queue rules.

It's the same story on a motorway. We've all been stuck in slow-moving traffic only to realise that the clown in front of you is in no rush to keep things moving. He's more than happy to leave a twenty-metre gap between him and the next car. You can't overtake him, because the other lane is blocked too, and you can't start honking the horn for fear of making the whole debacle even worse. He's taking things nice and easy, after all, it won't make it go any faster. But this isn't about speed; it's about keeping things moving so that your fellow motorist six miles back can take a morsel of comfort in the fact that we're not entirely in a stationary position. If everyone adopted the no-move rule, we'd simply be left with static queues everywhere.

A few months back, I was queuing for petrol. The queue had spilled onto the road. This was one of those enormous über-petrol stations where you can do a month's worth of shopping, browse a book section, pick up your parcels and stop by for a coffee along the way. Consequently, queue progress was a tad on the slow side.

The woman in front had adopted the big-gap policy. There was a good eight metres between her car and the one in front.

She was also about to commit queue crime number two; this one is exclusively the domain of the petrol station.

The rear end of my car was still hanging out into the road so I needed her to move forward as soon as she could. But she was going nowhere. Not until she had selected the petrol pump that she thought most likely to come free the soonest. This is a completely bonkers idea: you can't possibly know, from the comfort of your car, which customer is most likely to come back to their car first. It's like playing *Deal or No Deal* with fuel. The upshot is that as she waits to get lucky with the next available pump she has seventeen cars behind her and a completely empty expanse of forecourt in front.

Little did I know, as I waited for this halfwit to finally start moving, that she would be the same person who would go on to commit queue crime number three. This one happened inside the petrol station, as we all dutifully queued up to pay. Pump girl was no longer leaving a gap between her and the person in front (which was me); she was leaving no gap at all.

I guess we all have something of the ninja about us when it comes to knowing that someone is standing right behind us. Too close behind us. I could feel her breath, smell her perfume and hear the subtle chewing of gum. She was close, I'd say no more than a few centimetres away. I took a few shuffles forward as the queue began to move. This was surely her chance to recalibrate and stay where she was. But she moved too. Even closer. I could feel the gentle brush of her arm on the back of my jacket. This was insane. I briefly wondered if something else was going on here. Was she deliberately doing this? Was this a thing that some folk did for kicks while queuing up in the BP? Maybe there was a Facebook page where queue fetishists posted craftily taken snaps of blissfully unaware queuers being space-invaded in the name of some kind of proximity fixation. How can she *not* know what she is doing here? Her lips are virtually glued to the back of my neck – if I turned around, we'd be kissing. She'd just spent a good quarter of an hour dicking around on the forecourt, demanding enough space to stage a bullfight, and here she was virtually gearing up for the conga.

Queue Girl, Post Office Man and the dodgepot on the motorway are just three more entries on the growing league table of the blissfully unaware. Fellow mortals completely co-cooned and isolated from the existence of others. Considering we spend so much time at school being told how to queue nicely, it's extraordinary that this early life lesson has been so spectacularly removed from our inner code of conduct. Have we really reached a point in our evolution where we need to go back to basics and actually teach adults how to form a queue? Does this need to be part of the big tick list of life, like taking a driving test? That said, putting that into some kind of coherent action might be tricky:

'Could all of those who are here today for the queue lesson seminar, please form an orderly…'

56.

SUPERMARKET PIGGIES

It's not a café, it's a supermarket. It might have a café in it somewhere – at the front, probably, a place where you can go for a quick cuppa and an iced fancy post the big shop – but the shop itself *isn't* a café. Therefore you can't have your dinner in there by using the products on the shelves.

I'm convinced that this has become a self-perpetuating problem. Something people have heard about and therefore started to do. I'm almost sure that when I was a kid this would never have happened. It would have been up there with shoplifting itself. It *is* shoplifting. So who are the filthy thieves who think that grabbing grub off the shelves of your local supermarket, eating it, and then producing a bunch of empty packets at the till is acceptable behaviour?

I'm convinced this whole thing began with scuzzy parents doing it with their kids. Little Bella starts playing up and screaming like a banshee, so dad opens up some food he hasn't yet paid for to keep her quiet. We can always pay for it at the other end, he's thinking. Yes, you could do that, but the concept of this place is that you buy it first, and *then* pay for it. It was never designed to be a pacifying service for your loud kid.

At some point in time, this behaviour morphed into the adult world. Full-blown grown-ups nicking munch and eating it while they shop. Are these people really *that* hungry that they can't wait? Who are they? Is this the same mucky contingent who think nothing of going shopping in their pyjamas? Is it the same lot? Quite possibly. Regardless, you haven't got to walk up many aisles to see someone at it.

One man in my local Sainsbury's had the whole thing pretty much laid out on that little plastic flap on his trolley, where you would normally sit a child. Sandwiches, some chicken crisps and a bottle of Pepsi. He was actually having a picnic in his shopping trolley. He should have just brought his microwave along and knocked up a couple of ready meals. He was oblivious. And when he got to the till he simply presented a bunch of scrunched-up packages and labels. His face didn't at any point recognise that this is not the order of events.

The jury seems to be out as to whether this is illegal. Some shops apparently pull you up on it; others let it slide because most people do actually pay at the other end. But the issue does become a little more controversial when it comes to stuff you have to weigh, like fruit and veg. My man at the checkout tells me that it's not unusual for some sneaky little tea-leaf to turn up at the till with a polythene bag containing about six grapes.

You tend not to go into Next and stick on some boxers, a shirt, suit, socks and a pair of trainers and then ramp up to the cashier with five labels. There would be a conversation and a telling-off. You might even be banned from their stores for the crime of not behaving like an acceptable human being. And rightly so. So why does the weirdo subset think it's OK to do it with food?

How about we get a national campaign going to try to wean Brits back onto the path of decorum and decency and to teach confused shoppers that starvation can be avoided by simply eating before you go shopping? Huge billboards and flyers alike could send out the clear message of how to avoid pilfering from the food outlets simply by eating stuff before you walk in the place. Perhaps a government helpline, giving crucial advice on the dual horrors of theft and malnutrition, would help, alongside TV ads with Ant and Dec showing starving Brits tucking into their food before they embark on their weekly shop. Maybe Dr Hilary could add a health caveat imparting Brits to 'have a chop before you shop'.

Failing all of these ideas, just use the little café in the shop itself. I promise you, you won't waste away if you have to wait five more minutes before stuffing your face with a cheese toastie. You'll also have the added satisfaction of knowing that all your fellow shoppers no longer think you're a dicey little scum hound.

57.

HOTEL RECEPTIONISTS

Maybe it isn't specifically the fault of the receptionists, although I have my doubts. We live in an impressive world of automation and we are rightly encouraged to use the online world as much as we possibly can. After all, what could be simpler? Download an app and attend to all your worldly needs on your phone while lying in bed watching TV. There's now pretty much an abridged version for all nooks of life. Things that once took us ages to arrange, or involved reams of forms, are now neatly taken care of via a simple little box on your laptop or smartphone. The era of tech really is marvellous. Mostly.

I use a hotel maybe once a month. It's pretty much always work-related. The added beauty of using the same hotel is that each time I re-book, all the details are neatly saved online from the last time. I don't have to bother filling out my name and details; I just click 'Re-book', alter the dates, and I'm done. Thirty seconds later a little confirmation email comes flying into my inbox telling me that the manager and staff are looking forward to seeing me again. The world really is full of nice people.

'Good morning, sir. Nice to see you again,' says the beaming lady at the desk.

'Hi there, I have a booking, name of Collins. For one night.'

And so the fun starts. It's the same unfathomable pattern. The receptionist begins to get busy on the keyboard.

Tap, tap, tap, tap, tap, tap, tap, tap, tap, tap, tap, tap, tap, tap, tap, tap.

'Ian Collins?' she asks.

'Yes, that's me. Back again.' She smiles. I smile.

Tap, tap, tap, tap, tap, tap, tap, tap, tap, tap, tap, tap, tap, tap, tap, tap.

'For one night?' she asks without taking her eyes off the screen.

'Yes, one night.'

Tap, tap, tap, tap, tap, tap, tap, tap, tap, tap, tap, tap, tap, tap, tap, tap.

She's squinting a bit. I can see her eyes darting around the online form.

Tap, tap, tap, tap, tap, tap, tap, tap, tap, tap, tap, tap, tap, tap, tap, tap.

Now she's on mouse detail.

Click, click, click, click. Nearly there, surely.

Tap, tap, tap, tap, tap, tap, tap, tap, tap, tap, tap, tap, tap, tap, tap, tap.

'Have you stayed with us before?' Why is she asking me this? Wouldn't that info already be on the screen? In any case, does it matter?

'Many times.'

Tap, tap, tap, tap, tap, tap, tap, tap, tap, tap, tap, tap, tap, tap, tap, tap.

She pauses as she takes in her visuals. There's a vague look of confusion in her eyes.

Click, click, click.

'And you say it's just the one night?'

'Yep, still the one night.'

Tap, tap, tap, tap, tap, tap, tap, tap, tap, tap, tap, tap, tap, tap, tap, tap.

She looks up with what I assume is meant to be a reassuring smile. It doesn't reassure me.

Click, click, click. Tap, tap, tap. Click. We must be there by now.

'Do you have a car?' she asks.

'No car.' I'm now fed up.

Tap, tap, tap, tap, tap, tap, tap, tap, tap, tap, tap, tap, tap, tap, tap, tap. Click.

'Are you eating in the restaurant?'

'No.'

Click. Tap, tap, tap. Click.

She leans back a few inches, as if to assess the situation so far. Whatever she's looking at, she's clearly not done. This is a woman in deep concentration. Her head ducks a little as she re-examines her work. What is she doing on there? Is she simultaneously emailing her friends and organising a night out? Or perhaps finishing a particularly challenging Sudoku puzzle from earlier in the day? This is insane – there are more taps and clicks than there are questions. What is she doing? Am I booking in by instalments?

'Everything OK?' I ask.

'Yes, one moment.'

Tap, tap, tap, tap, tap, tap, click, click – tap, tap, tap, tap, tap, tap, tap, tap, tap, tap.

She takes a breath and stands back. Just one final thing. I

can see her mind turning over. Nearly there, surely. She reaches into a little box to obtain a white key card. Hallelujah. But she's not done. She inserts the card into a little machine. It makes a short, quiet buzz sound before she removes it.

Tap, tap, tap, tap, tap, tap, tap, tap, tap, tap, tap, tap, tap, tap, tap, tap. Click.

Again, she looks back at the screen.

'Do you want breakfast?' she asks.

'Yes, please. I wrote that down on the form.'

More clicks. More taps. She's done. She hands me the key card wrapped in a little paper wallet. She points me to the lift and explains that if there is anything I need then just press zero on the phone or come back to the reception. I resist the temptation to tell her that I wouldn't come back to the reception if the hotel and my own arse were on fire.

This pattern is repeated in hotels across the world. So what exactly was the point of my online check-in? What did I gain? Wasn't the whole idea of using the speedy app to bypass the very charade I have just been through? This entire process would have been no quicker had I walked in off the street and booked a room. The app, it seems, did nothing more than register my name. They knew I was coming, but that was it – everything else had to be officiously retyped and entered at their end. It was a ten-minute ball-ache, and not exactly conducive with the spirit of a one-click world.

I'm sure someone in the trade will one day explain why checking into a hotel – that you had already checked into – can take the best part of a quarter of an hour. I can't imagine what the hell is on that form that requires that amount of time to assign you a bed. My guess is that the hotel trade will concoct some yarn that they are compelled, by law, to add and click crucial data for consumer protection and customer safety, or some such nonsense. It's either that, or the more brutal reality that the job of a hotel receptionist is, for a large part, mind-numbingly boring and can leave employees with zero sense of urgency and the occasional propensity to not actually give a toss. Right now, my money is on the latter.

58.

IDIOTS WITH BOOKS

My mate Will is a sci-fi nut. He loves all that old pony. *Star Trek*, *Battlestar Galactica*, that thing with Ian McKellen and the Aussie actor and, of course, *Star Wars*. If Will isn't mentally in space at least twice a week, he starts to have palpitations. Which is how he came to tell me that he was re-watching the entire Lucas franchise on his way into work. On his phone. Now, I'm not a fully paid-up subscriber to The Force and I'm still royally confused about who is meant to be related to whom (Alec Guinness is R2-D2's dad, right?), but what I do know is that you can't watch *Star Wars* on an iPhone unless you have had a chromosome removed. *Star Wars* is a big-arse space movie and that requires some serious screenage. The whole experience is meant to bring you into a world of intergalactic hassle where mean men wear plastic hats and folk go nuts with illuminated snooker cues. The whole shebang begs you to be part of that journey and none of this can be achieved while watching it on a five-inch screen.

But in a world of a million box sets, busy Brits have decreed that the only way to stay bang up to date with everything pop culture-related is to cram in that viewing time while sitting on the train or bus to work. Will tells me that in his world, it's the only option. OK, I get it, it's not ideal, but it's a compromise. You might not be replicating the visual experience but at least you can still do it sitting down in a chair, vaguely relaxed.

The same cannot be said for the next group of gene-pool botherers. Like so many contemporary acts of absurdity, it's hard to pinpoint whether there was a specific time or moment when this one began. Regardless, you haven't got to have a PhD in people watching to know that the acts of walking, shopping, riding a bike or even driving a car are not activities that are compatible with reading a book. Just like swimming while eating or sitting on the loo while chatting to your mum, some things simply don't go together.

Surely the whole process of reading a book works in tandem with the act of relaxing? Isn't that kind of the point? If you took a *Family Fortunes*-type straw poll and asked one hundred people to name something you do while relaxing, reading a book would be right up there. People take a book to bed, they take one on holiday; in the summer they sit under a tree in the park and enjoy some relaxing rays while reading their favourite novel. Reading a book is pretty much the international symbol for a human in a state of relaxation. This is why we have libraries and reading rooms: the ambience and setting are conducive to concentration and relaxation. A bit of peace and quiet are kind of central to the act.

When I first read *The Great Gatsby*, I became so hooked on this incredible novel that I was ready to call into work and pull a sickie. The thing was glued to me like a second skin. But there was never a point when I wanted to take it shopping with me. Despite the magnetic nature of this bestselling page-turner,

I didn't once have the urge to walk down the street reading it. Not just because it is largely impractical to navigate any busy road with your fizzog buried into several hundred pages of a mighty classic, but because the whole charade is deeply incompatible with the enjoyment of reading.

I used to think it was a bit peculiar seeing people in the supermarket pushing a trolley while carrying out an animated phone conversation on a massive Bluetooth headset. Seeing fellow humans seemingly talking to themselves was a curious development. In retrospect, they look vaguely sane in comparison to their book-reading cousins. The sight of some loon doing a slalom down the fish aisle, almost taking out old folk and small people as he remains glued to his latest choice of fiction, is not one that comforts me when I consider the progress of the human journey so far.

Similarly, how the hell can you possibly read while walking along a busy road? It takes pretty much all of your instincts and faculties to remain alive on some of the UK's streets. Yet the sight of halfwits wandering along roads, utterly oblivious to cars and pedestrians because they're eyes-deep into a book is not uncommon. Whatever the obvious dangers, how could they possibly enjoy reading in these conditions?

Greater Manchester Police recently nicked a lorry driver for reading a book while travelling along the M60 (the guy was going full pelt while tucked into his latest tome), a cyclist in Warwickshire almost took out his own teeth when he smashed into the back of a car while reading, and a woman in the States walked off a pier into Lake Michigan while doing the same thing. Are they all reading the same damn novel? Is there some kind of Twilight Zone thing going on here where folk are being subliminally hypnotised into selecting certain titles that they can never put down?

In recent years we have become used to that irksome contingent who text while walking – the bozos who block doorways, randomly stop in the middle of the street and cross roads as cars hurtle towards them. The stats for bad accidents on this one are notching up every year. In one town in the US they have had so many major accidents that they are now considering making text-walking illegal. But the book club clowns have taken this moronic behaviour to even greater levels. Texting a message of 'See you later' to your mum is one thing; trying to read Dostoyevsky's finest while dodging a hundred vehicles is quite another.

Maybe naming and shaming is the only way. Perhaps we need one of those caught-on-camera YouTube moments where a book-reading cyclist collides with a book-reading driver who has narrowly missed a book-reading pedestrian. We can then sit back and watch the thing go viral. Perhaps then these clueless Herberts will finally realise that the best place to read a book is on a sofa. Not the A12.

59.

BUFFET MONSTERS

If you've never been to a Toby Carvery, please give it a spin. To coin a phrase, it's an experience. If you have even the slightest inclination to find out where you sit on the social spectrum, this is crucial research. Toby Carvery operate one of those 'all you can eat' policies. You pay your money and then queue up with 500 other people for some food. As you near the front, you grab a warm plate from the pile and wait your turn – like a school dinner queue for the grown-ups. As you near the counter, you get the first glimpse of what's on offer.

As fellow diners fill their plates, the breadth of choice is becoming apparent. Just a few more shuffles and you'll be there. Finally, you spy the booty – spread out like the Last Supper. A selection of meats so large and gleaming, they look like props from a Tim Burton movie. There's a massive turkey (do turkeys actually grow that big?), a four-stone lump of beef and a massive cube of ham. Guarding the meats is a chef-type character armed with a large knife and some kind of spear. He raises his eyebrows and asks which one you would prefer. One final scan and you make your decision. The man in the whites will then dutifully hack off your own body weight in your preferred choice. Slice upon slice is dispatched to your plate. You sense the plate drop slightly under its new-found weight. You smile and move on to Phase Two.

The veg and buffet section is impressive: parsnips, batons of carrots, broccoli and peas, spoons of swede, glazed chipolatas, bowl-sized Yorkshire puddings, cauliflower, cabbage, stuffing, sliced onions and spuds that look like cricket balls. The term 'all you can eat' was clearly coined as an advisory notice. It was never intended to be a legal instruction to eat all that you *can*. But the moment you reach that veg section, it all kicks off. It's like someone sounded a klaxon and, with all the chaos of a trading floor, Brits set to work like an army of industrial ants.

The challenge is set. A mêlée of arms and hands all stretching and reaching to scoop and spoon the maximum amount of food one can fit on a plate. As limbs interlock in the race for supremacy, puddings are stacked and veg is squashed in order to make up some extra plate space for more grub. Once in a while there's confusion in the pack as some of the supplies appear to be running low; just a few potatoes left, they need to be captured before the greedy git behind you has them for himself. He's clearly spotted them too. The fact that the chef has another 14,000 out the back is of no interest: this is about pride, now, and allowing a fellow diner that last spud just isn't the way these things work. Finally, your two-feet worth of food is almost complete. Only the gravy to go. You grab the jug and raise your arm to its maximum height, like you're about to water a mulberry bush; you then pour as if your hungry life depended on it. Job done.

The process then descends into something of a French farce as dozens of diners speedily interweave their way back to their tables with precarious towers of food without bumping or tripping. The fact that once they've sat down no one can actually see each other is of no consequence. For less than a tenner you have managed to pile the equivalent of eight Sunday dinners onto your plate. What's not to like?

The Toby Carvery is not alone in offering Brits the option of a week's worth of food in one hit. Chinese restaurants and hotel buffets are also guilty of the same thing. My in-depth research tells me that culinary sociologists are no nearer to explaining the buffet phenomenon. Is it a primal reaction to the very substance that keeps us alive or is this simply about base greed and the insatiable desire for a perceived freebie? Whatever is going on, it ain't pretty.

If you really do want to measure where you are on the evolutionary scale, nip down to Toby's. You can judge your place in the human pecking order based solely on the height of your stack of Yorkshires.

60.

PENGUINS

The title *67 People I'd Like to Slap* was always going to allow for some wiggle room. So let me have this one. Aside from anything else, if you're writing a list of things that get on every fibre of your nerves, not including penguins would be the mother of all errors.

How the hell have they got away with it for so long? Let's get this out the way right now: a penguin is *not* adorable. In that unwritten list of stuff we love about the animal world, this thing isn't ticking many boxes. A penguin is neither cute nor cuddly. It doesn't have that doe-eyed thing going on, it doesn't make funny squeaking noises, nor does it roll over if you tickle it under the chin. It doesn't bounce and gambol or play around with its friends. We marvel at big cats and elephants, orangutans and rabbits because we see life in those eyes: we see their purpose, their needs and desires, their strengths and vulnerabilities. A penguin has no such qualities. A penguin is just a shape in a sack. With two paddles glued to its side.

I'm pretty sure the penguins themselves were also coming to the uncomfortable realisation that the game was up. For years they had dined out on this wholly false idea that there was something fascinating and lovely about their very existence. They must have been laughing all the way to the next ice hole at how gullible the human race was to try to find a lovable quality in the chronically unlovable. They couldn't even fly, for God's sake, yet daft humans continued to dote. But behind closed penguin doors, they knew they were about to be rumbled. The penguins needed to take evasive action.

Their first foray into reinvention happened in the past century and came in the form of that chocolate bar deal. What better way to garner support than going for the kids card first. Kids love chocolate, so this was clearly going to be the easiest route back into the hearts and minds of a confused people. I'm still haunted by that suffocating sense of disappointment when an adult asked if you wanted a bar of chocolate only to produce a Penguin. I was holding out for a KitKat or a Wispa, but what did my nan give me? A flipping Penguin! This was like offering a child Ovaltine as a tasty beverage. A Penguin was *never* the real deal. But the ruse had clearly worked and the penguins had regained some love via the conduit of cocoa, sugar and a cartoon selfie on the wrapper. These Arctic hoodwinkers had re-secured their place on the big list of animals we quite like.

But as the next century dawned, the penguins needed a new initiative. Chocolate was now on the list of things *not* to like; it was unhealthy and no longer cool. They needed to think big. At penguin HQ, an executive decision was made. They needed to go to Hollywood.

If ever we needed confirmation that these waddling fruit loops were on the make, it came in the form of the worst documentary ever made. *March of the Penguins* is one of the greatest con jobs in cinema history since *Leaving Las Vegas*.

One or two mates had been to see the film and inaccurately informed me that it was worth a look. Against my better judgement, I took the plunge. Part of me was genuinely hoping that this was a chance to re-evaluate things, to quit my penguin hatred and finally fall in love with the world's ugliest bird. For those who haven't seen the doc, here's an abridged version: every year, 5,000 penguins walk from one part of the snow to another. They stand still for ages. The wind blows and the snow drifts. They have sex and then they walk back again. That's it. Seriously, that is it.

I'm pretty sure that when the executive producers saw the original edit, they too would have been scratching their heads wondering if it was missing something – an entire point, maybe. There would have been some high-level meetings and robust discussions. How can we make this work? We need some action in here, surely. Discombobulated studio bosses would have panicked. There must be more to penguin life that this old hooey. After much creative soul-searching, they came up with a sneaky plan. Why not get the bloke from *The Shawshank Redemption* to narrate it? Everyone loves Morgan Freeman.

And so Morgan was dragged into a voice booth to sex up a penguin flick with his low tones and soothing words. It was a nice try, but they were on a hiding to nothing. They would probably have had slightly more luck if they'd hired Stacey Solomon. The reality is: you can't make penguins interesting *or* entertaining. But it didn't matter. The studio had their product – a pseudo wildlife doc and a Hollywood A-lister. Viewers will just fill in the blanks and assume they are watching a work of genius. This was the emperor's new clothes of modern cinema.

And so the penguins lived another day. Shortly after the Freeman movie, the *Happy Feet* franchise hit the screens. The penguins had sealed the deal for several more generations of the chronically dupable. Doing phone-in shows for a living, I'm used to seeing a full switchboard of people wanting to talk about immigration and Brexit, crime and welfare. But where are the calls on the penguin con? How have my fellow humans swallowed this cutesy act for so long?

So let's have some brutal honesty here. Penguins are just rubbish. They are the Kardashians of the animal world: totally useless, serve no discernible purpose and we wouldn't notice or cry if they no longer existed. Some things really are this black and white.

61.

PARCEL DELIVERY CLOWNS

I recently made a fascinating discovery in my own garden. It was a lovely summer's day and I had taken the rare decision to get busy with the beds and borders. With a brand-new set of some big-arse clippers, I was on a mission. My knowledge of this gardening caper is pretty much zero. You could write what I know about horticulture on Alan Titchmarsh's elbow. But I do know that ivy is the enemy. Ivy is evil and not to be tolerated. If you see it, kill it. It's the ISIS of the plant world. My neighbour had allowed some of this green nonsense to grow uncontrollably from his fence into mine and it was now north bound, right up the side of my garden shed. I was about to bring its journey to an end.

I positioned myself for the kill, stretching my arms into the gap between the fence and the shed. My new shiny shears were doing the job nicely when I spotted something. Buried down by one of the fence posts, covered in weeds and mud, was a package. I did a brief double take. What the hell is this? I was searching for some kind of frame of reference. I scanned the garden. No one looking. I reached down to make the grab, pulling the package into the light. My mind was racing; the mixture of excitement and reservation. How long had it been there? Could it be something of value? What if it was the proceeds of a bank job that had needed to be momentarily hidden away until the thief could return safely? The package was soft and squidgy, weighing no more than a few pounds. I began to clean up the label area, looking for clues. And there it was. It was addressed to me. This felt like all shades of Twilight Zone. How could a parcel that was addressed to me end up wedged between a shed and a fence at the bottom of my garden? I noticed the date. The parcel was over six months old. Tentatively, I opened the package. And six pairs of socks fell out.

Everything clicked into place. I grabbed my phone and went back over my emails. I found it.

Dear Parcel People,

I recently ordered six pairs of socks from you. I paid for the next-day delivery option. They never arrived. Can you let me know if there was a problem?

They were very efficient at replying.

Dear Mr Collins,

Our driver tells us he did deliver your parcel and left it in a safe place. He also left a card to tell you this.

Right, he didn't leave a card, the lying swine. And what the hell is a safe place? Is this a game of hide and seek? Would it not have been consistent with basic logic and common sense to tell me *where* this safe place was? Was I meant to just keep searching for ever in the hope that I would eventually stumble upon my own socks? I could have searched for the next five years and never once have thought that the choice of *safe place* was wedging it between a shed and a fence. My garden has three bins and a storage box. None of them are locked and all would have been obvious places to put a parcel. At what point did this bozo walk in my back garden and think that his best plan of delivery action was to avoid all logical locations and hide it in a bush behind a shed?

The explosion in online shopping clearly means more parcels. Remember as a kid how exciting it was when an actual parcel turned up? Not just a letter but a proper parcel. The thrill of wondering what it could be was enormous. Today, parcels are just a pain in the arse. Across the UK, hundreds of thousands of them are landing on doorsteps by the minute. And it's fair to say that few are being delivered with the grace and efficiency of Postman Pat.

Anyone can now become a parcel delivery driver: it's one of those gig economy jobs where as long as you work eighteen hours a day you should achieve minimum wage. On top of that, we now have a proliferation of big companies all offering their services. How hard can it be? Here's a parcel, there's the house. You need to get item A to location B in a safe manner. That's it. But things have gone badly wrong at dispatch HQ.

I can't fully authenticate the following but it all seems rather plausible. Furthermore, and for wholly understandable reasons, I am unable to reveal my source. What I can tell you is that she's reliable. This is possibly the first time the official Delivery Rules of Doom have been made public. It makes for some grim reading. The following, I'm told, are the official guidelines for every parcel delivery driver in the UK.

1. When you knock on the door, knock as loud as you possibly can in order to signal to the homeowner that some kind of massive emergency is taking place right outside. Do not leave a pause before knocking a second time, and equally as loud. Where possible, try to ring the bell simultaneously.

2. If you are feeling a bit tired and you can't be arsed to knock, ignore Rule 1 altogether and just chuck the parcel over their fence. Pay no attention to how delicate it might be. Just imagine you're a shot-putter and give it some serious muscle as you propel the thing into the backyard.

3. Always leave a note. The note could say that the parcel will be left with a neighbour or it might say that you have left it in a safe place. Ideally, write down where that safe place is, but, if your hand is aching from all that writing, don't make any reference to its location at all. Alternatively, a completely blank note, with no information on it whatsoever, is also fine.

4. If you are in a bit of a rush and need a fag break, ignore Rule 4 and don't leave a note at all. The homeowner will just assume they have mislaid it.

5. Where possible, try to leave the parcel in a recycling bin on the same day that the recycling people show up.

6. Try to hide the parcel in the last place anyone with a brain would think of looking.

7. If it's raining very, very hard, try to leave the parcel in the most exposed place you can find. At all costs, you must avoid looking for a nice dry location.

8. If at any point you sense that the parcel contains an item of value that could reap some serious cash if sold on eBay, then don't deliver the parcel at all. Just nick it.

You begin to see what a national crisis this is. Right across the country we have parcels missing, damaged, misplaced or trousered on a daily basis. Brits are beside themselves with woe. So, if you do come home and are convinced the parcel folk should have delivered your new purchases but can't seem to find any evidence of them, don't bother ringing a five-quid-a-minute helpline, just grab yourself a spade and try digging up your front lawn, just in case some enterprising halfwit has decided that a safe place meant burying the thing six feet under.

62.

COUNCIL CHIEFS

We never stop banging on about the bankers. The dirty thieves nicked our money. We should never let it go. MPs are no better: this pack of double-dealing dodgepots have been stealing our cash for years in the name of flatscreen TVs and duck houses. Public life, it seems, can be a grubby business. But while we have been banging on about these treacherous acts of theft and venality, we have totally taken our eye off the ball of *local* government. Forget the boys and girls at Westminster or the coke heads in the City: if you want to see larceny on an epic scale, look no further than your own backyard.

Curiously, we tend to see local authorities almost in the same way we see charities. They look after parks and playgroups, swimming pools and libraries. They tend to roads and flower beds. Every month we dutifully pay our local taxes in order to make it all happen. We do our bit and, in return, our local authority does theirs. All very civilised. We just don't tend to view these local guys with quite the same suspicious eye as we do their national counterparts. It would surely be unthinkable to imagine that your local town hall is merely another tier of bureaucracy crammed full of viciously ambitious politicians and public servants with PhDs in how to waste money. Time for a swift rethink.

The most blatant example of the upside-down world of local government comes courtesy of the council chiefs who earn more than the Prime Minister. You don't need to know much about either maths or politics to know that something has gone absurdly wrong when the person who makes decisions about where to build roundabouts is earning more than one who decides on the future of the country's nuclear deterrent. Who is crunching the numbers here – Bernie Madoff? The British Prime Minister earns £140,000 a year. The head of Surrey County Council earns £220,000. What happened? Is there no overlord of government finances checking this stuff? Fellow councillors have to give these vitally important decisions the thumbs-up; doesn't one of them raise a suspicious eyebrow that this might just be a smidgen over the top when it comes to the delicate issue of how to spend other people's money?

When challenged, the wagons circle. The last thing your local authority wants is pesky taxpayers getting all self-righteous. The only answer that ever comes back from the council bat cave is that if you want quality, you have to pay for it. If they didn't stump up the going rate, these nifty council super-servants would simply up sticks and go and work in the private sector. With respect, this is bollocks. Most of these luck merchants wouldn't know what to do in the private sector if they were injected with James Dyson's DNA. These guys are institutionalised local government monkeys who have drifted from one local authority job to another all of their professional lives. They're going nowhere.

The number of these freeloaders now earning the same as or more than the PM runs into tens of thousands. Their impressive pay packets and pension pots can be found in few other fields. Yet despite their austerity plans of cutting back on adult social care, children's centres and anything that might be helpful to someone with no legs, their own impressive stash remains untouched. Even losing your job in these places is a gift. It's a known fact in public life that if you want to see seventeen senior council employees writhing and convulsing with joy, just tell them the redundancy notices are on the way.

Whatever guff they give out about the dire need to save cash, when it comes to discharging one of their own, the telephone number-like remuneration packages would make the boys from Enron blush. A P45 in the world of public service is akin to the lotto jackpot. This invariably means a six-figure tax-free lump sum (how is *anything* tax-free?) and a cheeky six-figure top-up on the already six-figure pension pot. All nicely financed by pensioners and those on minimum wage. And if you want an extra kick in the cojones, it won't take much of a Google search to see how many of these loyal public servants were forced to walk the plank in circumstances that are literally criminal.

And there's one final conundrum to mess with our heads. Not a week goes by when you can't find a PM-type salary gig going in local government. *The Guardian*'s pages are full of them. From chief execs to quota alliance implication managers, through to the principal head of stuff (you will need a Freedom of Information request to see exactly what these *public* servants actually do all day), there's a litany of extremely important jobs to fill. And who usually fills them? Step forward the very people who have just been kicked out of another local authority. So we end up with the ludicrous situation where a public servant has been given a walk-away package of half a million quid from one local authority only to walk back into an identical gig in another. And with the very same towering pay packet. Holy Mother of Moses, where the hell is the Civic Director of Reasonableness when you need him?

These kind of cosy, unmonitored arrangements and ruses are going on daily. From wages and expenses to hospitality, perks and pay-offs, the chieftains down there at your local town hall are shameless. When it comes to government employees playing fast and loose with public money, these guys would give the People's Republic of Uzbekistan a run for its money any day of the week.

63.

CASHPOINT PHOBICS

The latter part of the twentieth century brought us all manner of tech-based advancements in the world of 'how to make human existence a whole lot easier than it used to be'. Previous generations would have either marvelled or run for the hills in terror at how automation has become key to the human journey. From turning over the telly channels with a little black box, to opening car windows at the touch of a button, to fridge-looking devices that clean plates and cutlery. From the 1960s onwards, life simply got a whole lot easier. And then there was John Shepherd-Barron, the inventor of the cash machine.

It is perhaps a minor crime that Shepherd-Barron is not a household name. While many of his contemporaries went on to become as famous as the very things they invented, John stayed relatively anonymous. Despite the international impact of his endeavours, even the collective brains of TV's *Eggheads* would struggle to identify this modest Scot and what he gave to the world.

You might have imagined that it was the Yanks who gave us cash machines. The Americans were using credit cards and buying things on finance when the UK had only just dispensed with ration books. If anyone was going to find a way to get cash out of a brick wall, it was surely our American cousins. But it fell to John to put the gubbins together and conjure up a device that has totally revolutionised the way humans do business.

In June 1967, a branch of Barclays Bank in Enfield, north London, was the proud location of Planet Earth's first ever cash machine. The world's press dutifully gathered in order to record this most radical of breakthroughs in personal financial freedom. Clearly, this was a major event and it was therefore vital that the right person was chosen to unveil this monumental landmark in global technology. The decision process must have been tough.

Did they go for James Callaghan, the British Prime Minister? Maybe George Woods, the then head of the World Bank? Or perhaps they would just go for the bullseye and ask the Queen. In the end, none of these got the gig. Whatever passed for a PR company back in 1967 decided that they would go for an altogether different vibe. The job of unveiling the world's first ever cash machine fell to Reg Varney.

For those who weren't around back then (me included) or aren't fully au fait with the history of British popular culture, Reg was an actor, most famed for his role in a very shit sitcom called *On the Buses* (once in a while, ITV3 will still show the film version). *On the Buses*, like many back then, was a fairly route-one affair where overt sexism and mild racism formed the backbone of every episode. Reg was a bus driver, lived at home with his mum and got himself into all sorts of scrapes and predicaments that invariably ended with him slapping the arse of a female conductor before romping with her on the back seat of a No. 352. Reg's slap-and-tickle shenanigans were then brought to an untimely halt by the inspector, who took a very dim view of his capers and vowed to 'get him' next time he was caught using company time to canoodle with a woman about forty years his junior. Roll the titles.

Reg was probably about as famous as an actor could be back then, so I guess from a profile perspective it made sense. In every other respect, it was a pretty bonkers idea. I can't help but wonder whether, if they had drafted in someone else – some kind of monetary type – the nation might have taken the whole thing a bit more seriously and fifty years up the road Brits would be a tad more au fait with how to use the hole in the wall. By now, using a cash machine should be as effortless as tying your shoelaces. But for reasons I've yet to get to the bottom of, this pretty rudimentary piece of tech is still discombobulating customers on an almost minute-by-minute basis. There's confusion in the ranks.

The sign on the machine says Fast Cash. It's a clue. The subtext (as if one is needed) is that the process you are about to undertake will be a pretty swift affair. Done and dusted within seconds. A few taps of the keys and you'll be out of there, walking back up the road with thirty quid in your back pocket, all courtesy of Mr Shepherd-Barron's innovative brilliance. But our trusty inventor hadn't factored in the un-predictable nature of what happens when man meets machine. In particular, a phenomenon which can only be described as Screen Stare.

You're second in the queue but this shouldn't be a problem. Being twentieth in a cash machine line *is* an issue – you're there for the long haul. Being second is fine. The person in front has their card at the ready, so all being well you'll be done within forty seconds and on your way. But hang on there, something is afoot. Your co-customer has stalled at the first hurdle. What is he doing? He's got his card ready to go but he appears to be studying the screen. What is he looking at? There's nothing to see, the screen is merely inviting you to insert your card. Come on, buddy, you can do it – whack it in there. He's wavering some more. Now he's nibbling the corner of his card, still pondering the screen. You can do it, it's just a quick insertion and you're onto step two. His hand moves slowly towards the point of entry. You peek over his shoulder, just in case you're missing something – have Santander decided to show an episode of *EastEnders* prior to cash withdrawal? What's the delay? Screen Stare has clearly kicked in. Finally, the satisfying click and buzz as the machine receives his card.

The dilly-dallying on step two is almost at criminal levels. Yes, I know it's annoying when an inanimate object wants to ask you lots of questions: do you want to check your balance first, would you would like a receipt, do you require another transaction etc., but it's all pretty straightforward – three taps and you should be on your way. But our man is dithering again. How long can it take to decide if you want twenty quid or a hundred? He's unsure. His finger wavers over the various options. Does he think it's a quiz? Is he worried that if he gets it wrong a giant boxing glove will smash through the screen and smack him one up the bracket? Eventually he settles for a tidy thirty. Not long now. The machine does its brief calculations and dispenses his card. Now stand by for Screen Stare part three.

Our man is not done. He has his card and his money but is clearly under the impression that there's something more to this process. He puts his card and cash back into his pocket, but his eyes never leave the screen. He's scanning the tiny monitor. What is he actually doing? Does he think there's a Monday special on – a two-for-one deal when you make a withdrawal? He takes a small step towards completion but continues his gaze. What the frick is he looking at? There's literally nothing to see. He steps away but takes one final look over his shoulder, just to be sure. A transaction that should have taken forty seconds has just taken three minutes.

I reckon each town loses about five weeks' worth of productivity because of the Cashpoint Screen Stare. This is a sizeable dent in the public coffers. This isn't how it was meant to be. Mr Shepherd-Barron may well have been ahead of the game but clearly it wasn't quite enough. We now need to employ the next tier of innovation to stop blissfully unaware numpties eating into the lunch hours of decent Brits who just need a tenner for a sandwich.

Maybe the boxing glove idea isn't too ridiculous after all. Or perhaps we should bolt giant egg timers to the sides of all cashpoints; failure to transact within the allotted period means your balance is wiped clean. Failing that, we just get the woman who does the supermarket checkout voices to record an 'unexpected dickhead at the cash machine' line. It is now the twenty-first century, after all.

64.

FOLK WHO CLAIM THEY CAN TALK TO THE DEAD

At this point in the twenty-first century, I should be able to write something like:

> Until recently, some people thought you could communicate with the dead. Gullible humans used to book and pay actual cash to other humans in exchange for messages and directives from the other side. They thought that dead relatives would rise from the grave to pass on reassuring words and inform the bereaved that despite their untimely demise, all was fine and dandy in their post-death paradise.

But the words still stand. I did some cursory research online to get a rough idea of how many people are peddling their wares in the name of psychic communication. If you tap in 'Free Psychic Readings UK', almost 6 million results pop up. And when you drill down, none of them are free. The psychic industry has never been bigger.

My mate Al had been invited by a neighbour to go to a psychic evening at her house. They had invited along a local clairvoyant to carry out the readings. Her credentials had claimed that she was one of the best at getting in touch with folk who were very much dead. *One* of the best? Is there a gradient of ability going on here? I would have thought that this is very much something you either can or can't do – surely you have the gift or you don't? Being *one* of the best suggests a pecking order.

Maybe there's a paranormal league table that we are not privy to. Perhaps there are the Manchester Uniteds of the psychic world at one end, those who can impart long, detailed conversations from the other side, while at the lower end we have the Shrewsbury Town types who only manage to pass on the odd grunt from Grandad or a vague meow from your dead cat. Either way, this woman claimed to be up there in the higher echelons of supernatural communicators.

The scene was set. Twenty people all gathered in the living room of No. 56. Psychic Sarah was placed in the dining room. She needed a more solitary location in order to get the vibes going. One by one, each person was called through for their own personal reading. Eventually, Al took the walk of psychic joy. Sarah was waiting, looking all serene and wise.

'*Stop,*' said Sarah out of nowhere, before Al had a chance to sit down. 'You have come to me at a difficult time. I have news for you.'

Stone the crows, Al hadn't even got his feet under the table and she was already getting some nudges from the spirits. She inhaled deeply and gestured for Al to take a seat.

'You have come to me for reason and purpose. I have many who would like to talk with you. They have things to say.'

'Thank you very much,' said Al. Sometimes there really is no other answer.

'Would you like me to record the reading?' she asked, help-fully. 'You will then have a record for the rest of time.'

Al nodded.

'Pass me your phone,' said psychic Sarah. 'It's important that you don't forget what I tell you. The spirits need you to remember their messages. Tonight is your night, Al. Tonight I will guide you. Please don't be scared, the people who care about you are with us right now.'

Sarah looked down towards the table. Her shoulders began to move up and down as if being worked by strings. Her breath became more rapid. She seemed to be going into some kind of trance. The spirits had clearly arrived. She looked up at Al with a stare that could have downed a small mammal.

'I'm ready to begin,' said Sarah, in a slightly deeper tone than before. She hit the record button on the phone and placed it back onto the table.

'Who is Jerry?' said psychic Sarah.

Al almost fell off the chair. His mouth was as dry as sand.

'Jerry is…'

'…one of your best friends?' interrupted the Witch.

'Yes, he is.'

'He looks out for you, Al. The spirits are telling me that he is close to you right now. He is your guide here on earth?'

Al nodded. He was gobsmacked. And scared. Her opening gambit was a straight bullseye.

'The project will come together,' said Sarah, out of nowhere. 'Does that mean something to you?'

Al was dumfounded. He nodded again. Him and his mate Jerry had been putting together a proposal for a business idea they had. They had been working on it that very day.

'The spirits are telling me that you have no need to worry. You and Jerry are a good partnership. Things will happen. Please stay calm.'

Al smiled and struggled to hold back a tear. He had dissed this kind of psychic nonsense for years, pooh-poohing any suggestion that this sort of hokum could ever be possible. Yet here he was in a dining room just off Bromley High Street getting direct and accurate messages via the dead. God knows what she's going to say next. He was about to get the answer.

'Let's move on,' said psychic Sarah. 'I'm now hearing directly from your most recently departed.' She swayed her head from side to side as if trying to tune in to the spirits. Her face adopted a more forlorn look.

'Was it Aids?' she asked.

'Sorry?' replied Al.

'Aids. Your partner, did he die of Aids?'

This was tricky. Al wasn't really here to try to make contact with a dead partner. Mainly because there was no dead partner. And then there was the other issue. Al isn't gay. His partner wouldn't be a *he* anyway. Who was she getting in touch with here, Liberace?

'Er, no,' said Al. 'Doesn't really…'

Sarah jumped in. 'I'm getting an old lady…'

That's more like it, thought Al. He'd only come out of politeness to his neighbour, but had kept in mind that if this charade threw up a bit of a chinwag with his old nan, then it would be a nice bonus.

'That could be my nan,' said Al, too helpfully.

'She's worried about the amount you're drinking. She's says you need to lay off the vodka, it'll kill you.'

Al is a teetotaller.

'She's worried that you're letting yourself go and not keeping the place tidy. She says you can't go on living in that mess.'

It's genuinely quite difficult to find enough superlatives to describe just how tidy a person my mate Al is. He's pretty much OCD when it comes to cleanliness and hygiene. You could confidently carry out surgery on his kitchen floor with no chance of infection. But here was Derek Acorah's love child telling him in no uncertain terms that his 'nan' has concerns about his ability to keep his house spick and span. On top of that, she thinks he's a pisshead, despite him having never drunk in his life.

The reasons for Sarah's catalogue of supernatural errors is all rather simple: she's a fraud. A total charlatan. I've done countless phone-ins on this issue and even had psychics live in the studio giving often desperate callers a personalised reading. It's quite something to see them in action. They duck, dive and dart in all directions before settling on what they think the recipient will recognise. Once on a theme or a name, they'll play out this technique for all it's worth, leaving a grateful caller remembering the 10 per cent of things that they half recognise but subconsciously forgetting the 90 per cent that meant nothing. It's called cold reading: the ability to create the impression, via word play and encouragement, that they know more than you actually do.

What happened with Al was even more galling. Turns out that the only reason she was able to pinpoint Jerry as his guiding hand on Planet Earth was because she had read his text messages. While psychic Sarah was lining up Al's phone to record the event, she simply had a peek at his last bunch of texts and then relayed the salient points. Even Doris Stokes would have taken a dim view of that one.

Psychic Sarah left Bromley that night with a thousand quid in her purse. Not a bad rate for four hours' worth of total bullshit. She's one of a gazillion quack merchants throughout the UK purporting to talk to the dead and give spiritual guidance via the conduit of a paranormal gift. In order to keep pace with entrepreneurial norms, they now offer even more ways to rob you blind: you can have readings on the phone, by text or even on Twitter. They also offer a variety of options from rune stones to tea leaves, tarot cards to palms. The choice is yours.

If you ever have a spare fifty quid and one of these psychic sorts comes-a-peddling, smile politely before telling them to shove their crystal ball up their mystical arse. Stick your cash on a horse instead: at least you know it exists and you might even get some money back.

65.

PEOPLE WHO HATE NICK CLEGG

Hear me out.

Hating the Tories is a rite of passage; even when we think they're right, there's an in-built alarm system within us that dictates that we must still say they are wrong. Even if they come up with a policy that is clearly identical to the one from the party we do support, we must still insist they are off the mark. Hating Tories is simply a national sport, so let's not upset the apple cart. Similarly, having a pop at Labour for being a bunch of whippet-owning dodge merchants who want to spend all your money on daft diversity projects and indoctrinate the nation's children with an irrational love of Cuba is also a fairly healthy approach to life.

But we never had any of these stereotypical or irrational views of the Liberal Democrats. The Lib Dems were that political enigma that sat almost mute on the back benches while the two main parties battled it out. Once in a while they would surface for a bit of scrap at PMQs, but, for the most part, these fifty or so, mostly leftist, MPs remained schtum for several decades. None of us had a bloody clue who any of them were.

And then, out of flipping nowhere, they became the government. And it all went tits up.

Whatever worthy ideas the Lib Dems had strewn across their manifesto, it was the delicate matter of free tuition fees for all that caused all the hassle. This was mainly due to the slightly awkward fact that the Lib Dems had no intention of giving free tuition fees to anyone. Notionally, they liked the idea (who doesn't like free stuff?), but given there was zero chance that our silent friends would ever be in a position of power, they were in a pretty safe place to very publicly advocate tuition fees as an aspirational freebie.

The whole point of coalition government is that it involves both compromise and abandonment of policy. That's kind of the way it's meant to work. The only way it can work. Hard-working Tory MPs and their party workers who had dutifully pounded the streets handing out leaflets promising all manner of blue-based ideas now had to look constituents in the eye and tell them that many of their pledges simply weren't going to happen. David Cameron had to hit the dispatch box knowing that almost half his manifesto was never going to see the light of day. No one blinked. There was no public outcry claiming Conservative duplicity when they were forced to abandon their pledges on prison reform and the UK courts, and not a single newspaper front page went nuts on their failed pledge to cut stamp duty.

Yet, at the same time, Nick Clegg was being publicly crucified for his callous abandonment of their higher education pledge. It wasn't only students who wanted his blood; the entire political establishment and most of the public wanted a few drops too. Not a week passed over a five-year period when

Clegg didn't get an almighty lashing for his wicked lies. The fact that this was a coalition and compromise was actually the way it had to be counted for sod all. Nick Clegg was a lying arse who should be castigated for the rest of time. Effigies were made of him on Bonfire Night, extra security had to be drafted in to protect him, and Lib Dem members even quit the party in disgust. On the plus side, this was the defining moment when we could, once and for all, conclude that Liberal Democrats really were the political moon-howlers of our times. A party that had been in perpetual opposition for a billion years had finally – and against *all* odds – made it into government and its own members were legging it like lemmings. To compound this madness, many were going off to join the Labour Party, the very party who introduced tuition fees in the first place.

What hadn't helped matters was that Clegg & Co. had made the fees issue such a high-profile policy in the run-up to 2010. They were obsessed. Their front bench had even taken to signing personalised agreements with students and then posing for the press clinging onto giant cardboard contracts, grinning like terrified lottery winners. Yet while uni fees were a weighty issue, in the grander scale, there were far bigger ones. Ask a hundred people to name ten things that are very important in public life – it's unlikely that student fees would make the list. Yet this relatively minor policy was enough to bury Clegg and send his party into political oblivion.

It's beyond surreal. In 2010, Nick Clegg had just fifty-seven MPs and yet they managed to get 75 per cent of their manifesto into government policy, fighting off the dominating Tories at every level. This should place the Lib Dems as one of the greatest political success stories in modern history and Nick

Clegg one of the greatest leaders of our times. In the follow-up election, they were wiped out. Even some of their own members didn't vote for them. Today they have just nine MPs and their time in office is as distant a memory as England winning the World Cup.

In the real world, Nick Clegg should be spoken of in the kind of reverential terms we reserve for Asquith and Lloyd George. Today, his public image sits somewhere between Neil Kinnock and Mr Tumble. This is not a good place to be. The only lessons I can perm from this farce are that most armchair pundits really are stupid and that Lib Dem voters are psychopathic wackjobs who you shouldn't trust out the back cutting the grass. On everything else, I agree with Nick.

66.

THE *QUESTION TIME* AUDIENCE

British TV audiences never used to clap and whoop like the American lot. We used to have programmes in this country presented by the likes of Clive James, who gave us a unique glimpse of what Yankee TV looked like. Pre-multi-channel telly, this was the only opportunity we got to see what happened across the pond. As a kid, this fascinated me. It also scared me. Why do the audiences keep clapping? It didn't matter what was happening, they just clapped. Like demented sea lions, they clapped and hollered as if their lives depended on it, all because a guest on *The Tonight Show* had just announced that they were born in Denver. Why are they clapping a place name? A contestant on *Wheel of Fortune* has just told the host she's at university studying sports science and the audience has exploded as if she's just announced that she's going to run for the Oval Office. Meanwhile on *The Phil Donahue Show* a man just revealed that he's a postman and the audience went nuts. Why are they doing this?

Back in the UK, we had no such cacophonous nonsense. We were far more laid-back and conservative. Any guest pitching up on *Parky* got a polite smattering of applause and that was it. If they wanted any more, they could whistle.

At some point, this all changed. I'm tempted to blame *Stars in their Eyes*, or *Gladiators*. I'm pretty sure it was around that mid-'90s era when it all went pear-shaped and Brit audiences began to adopt the same irrational and utterly mental responses to any old flannel said by a guest or contestant on a TV show. It's now a staple reaction on any light entertainment programme that audiences work themselves into a heart attack-inducing frenzy based on pretty much bugger all.

But then something *really* damn odd started to happen. Audiences began applying a version of this reaction to current affairs. Political debate programmes, news-based panel shows and even one-to-one interviews – wherever there was a live audience, an irrational, collective din wasn't far away.

The biggest offender is *Question Time*, the BBC's flagship political discussion programme. If any show should have swerved this pantomime farce then surely this was the one. Sadly for Mr Dimbleby & Co., it wasn't to be and *Question Time* audiences are now pretty much interchangeable with those who pitch up on the live final of *Big Brother*.

So what exactly prompts an audience to go crackers? There's a formula at work here, a sequence of events, cues or moments that make the audience squawk and boo, or cheer and clap. I think I've cracked the code. Here, for the first time, I can reveal the official blueprint for what makes a *Question Time* audience tick.

For the audience, it's a rare moment to be seen on the telly. Friends and family are watching. so straight away there's an in-built instinct to want to attach themselves to all the nice things the panel might have to say. The last thing they want is the neighbours at No. 37 seeing them giving enthusiastic applause to Nigel Farage's immigration policy, no matter how much they might agree with it. Much nicer for community cohesion to be seen bellowing like a fish wife.

Then there's the non-political guest on the panel, usually a comedian or a writer. These guys are a clear, safe bet for some alignment. Plus they're usually funny. This week it's Ian Hislop.

'I think our entire system needs changing. All you lot [pointing to the three politicians] are in it together. None of you have made any effort to really clean up politics in this country.'

This is intoxicating stuff for the audience. The applause and cheers are off the scale. There's even some stamping of feet. Who could possibly disagree with the statement that politicians need to be better at stuff? Genius.

Next up is the MP representing the government of the day. This one is always a battle. We hate governments, even if we agree with them. Especially when we see them on the telly. Iain Duncan Smith is about to give a defence of welfare reform and, let's be honest, he's on a hiding to nothing; IDS couldn't get a round of applause if he'd just rescued a drowning puppy. He wasn't even halfway through when the disquiet began. There were mumblings and low boos coming from the back. Lucifer had spoken. As the former minister gave his thoughts on millionaire OAPs getting bus passes, you could hear the villagers lighting their torches. This man was ripe for a lynching.

IDS was doing his best, but the howls of disapproval were too much. Dimbleby had to step in – no one disobeys the mighty Dave, surely. As the quiet man completed his answer, the crowd finally turned. The BBC sound department adjusted their mic levels accordingly. The boos and jeers could be heard as far as Sheffield, which was quite something considering this episode was being recorded in Penzance. A lone shout of 'You're a disgrace' could be heard through the babble. You don't get this much audience participation in *The Rocky Horror Show*. IDS took it on the chin and the audience looked more than pleased with their collective response. Who doesn't want to be seen publicly kicking the arse of Iain Duncan Smith?

The member of the Green Party then pitches in to compound the torment, stating that Iain Duncan Smith is responsible for more misery than the great plague. Under normal circumstances, a member of the Green Party would simply be ignored, but this is telly, damn it, and she's saying something that sounds as if she's on the north end of nice, so what's not to like? The audience barks their approval and gives a prolonged cheer to their new-found ally. Someone at the back even whistles.

Dimbleby has had enough bickering from the panel. He wants to hear what the audience has to say. The *real* people. If you ever find yourself being part of the *QT* audience, here are the top five instant routes to hero status from your fellow audience members. Any of the following will guarantee you a whooping so loud it'll be heard on the northern craters of Mercury.

1. HAVE A DIRECT GO AT ONE OF THE PANEL.

This is bread-and-butter stuff in the audience endorsement department. It doesn't really matter which side of the argument you are on. The mere fact that a lowly member of Her Majesty's public has a right royal dig at a senior Cabinet minister is enough to buy the crowd. If you can throw in phrases like 'you're out of touch' or 'you all lie' and especially 'you try living on the minimum wage', extra house points are guaranteed.

2. SPEAK LOUDLY.

Dramatics work. If you haven't got an especially good point to make, don't worry, just raise your voice – it'll give a dramatic sense of indignation and the audience will love it. Try some meaningless phrases like 'I am fed up with politicians telling me how to live my life' – this kind of vacuous guff is a winner when said in a very loud voice.

3. SPEAK BADLY.

Whether it's an accent issue or you're just prone to mumbling, it doesn't matter – the audience will love you. Nothing the crowd likes more than to be seen supporting the person who is struggling with their words, it's a banker. The fact that it might take you almost half the programme to spew out your point is of no relevance.

4. END ON A CRESCENDO.

Regardless of what you're trying to say, just make sure you give it large on the last sentence. Think McKellen at the National and you'll get the idea. If you can build those final words into a frenzy of outrage '...WE-HAVE-HAD-ENOUGH' – and simultaneously point your finger, you'll be adored for the rest of time.

5. MENTION THE BANKERS.

• • •

Any of the above will guarantee you hero status in the room. Social media will love you ('Just watched a man totally destroy IDS on Question Time, RT') and you'll be left with a nifty video on your phone for whenever you and your mates start talking about Andy Warhol's fifteen minutes. You can't go wrong.

I'm not sure how we have spectacularly managed to lose our sense of decorum on these matters but watching *Question Time* is now up there with an episode of *The Price is Right*. Surely it can't be long before the pew-dwelling massive on *Songs of Praise* take up the cudgels and start lobbing rotten veg at Aled Jones the moment he knocks out that *Snowman* number.

67.

MIDDLE-CLASS TWENTY-SOMETHINGS

If you're in your twenties and from a nice middle-class background, you will never be skint. Assuming you haven't fallen out with your entire family, you're sorted. For life.

Here's how it works. There's a brutal reality out there right now: young people can't get on the property ladder. Rents are too high and houses too expensive. Even if you do find a place that's remotely affordable, the deposit required makes the whole thing pretty much impossible (a deposit which twenty years earlier would no doubt have purchased the entire house). The upshot is that millions of young folk will be living with their parents until they are eighty-two.

But there's a whole other demographic who are completely insulated from this whole farce. If you're a child of the '80s or '90s, from a cosy middle-class background, the chances are your grandparents were among the first generation to have purchased a house. It probably cost them about three quid and the mortgage was paid off many years before you were born. The conventional order of events suggests that your mum and dad would also have been homeowners from the off and possibly have paid off their mortgage too. Just to add to this impressive picture of prudence, it's a fair bet that both your parents and your grandparents will also have squirrelled away a good few quid along the way. Not to put too fine a point on it, but right now, you're sitting on a fricking goldmine.

I've lost count of the number of times I've heard mates in that age bracket moaning and bleating because there's no chance they can ever buy a house. Newsflash: you won't ever have to – you've got a couple coming your way for free. Forget the idea of having to save any dosh or going easy on those nights out – half a million quid's worth of bricks and mortar will be landing in your lap before you know it.

I took a call on the show recently from Seb in Chelsea.

'Our generation is the first to be worse off than our parents,' he sighed.

'What do your parents do for a living, Seb?'

'My dad's a GP and my mum is a head teacher.'

'Thanks for your call.'

Click.

I don't want to sound harsh, but poor old Seb didn't get it. I'm not suggesting he should be wishing away the days until his folks and grandparents bugger off to the big gates, but it must have crossed his mind that at some point he'll be on the receiving end of a significant legacy. Assuming his gran hasn't bequeathed all her worldly goods to the local cattery, or he hasn't upset her by giving her a Cradle of Filth album for Christmas, Seb and his siblings are on target for some free money. Years down the line, the same scenario will be repeated with his own parents. Seb will never need a mortgage or a pension.

I recently spoke to a guy on the show who had inherited four houses within nine years. He'd come from a line of one-child families which left him as the ultimate beneficiary of the entire empire. By the time he was thirty-eight, he was a millionaire twice over. And he didn't have to lift a finger. This might well be an extreme case and clearly he would rather not have ended up here in the first place, but the point stands.

The UK is on target to produce millions of people from similar backgrounds, all of whom will be secure enough to retire by the time they hit their mid-forties. Has the world of economics not come up with a name for this inevitable phenomenon? And why hasn't Martin Lewis started a page on his website especially for this eventuality? We are just years away from a whole new world where swathes of semi-posh folk mooch aimlessly around the place with no discernible purpose other than visiting nail bars and coffee shops and taking up bowls twenty-five years earlier than is healthy, and the *FT* aren't even talking about it.

Next time the plight of young people and their inability to pay for a roof over their own heads crops up, it's just possible they're not actually talking about you; the Bank of Mum and Dad fraternity are not included in this one, so quit your moaning. Unless your folks are utter bastards, life will pan out just nicely. If you have to live in that box room in Clapham for a few more years, don't panic: happy days of comfort clothes and gardening are a mere decade away.

EPILOGUE

I said at the beginning that this will be an unarguable list of stuff that drives you up the wall. I trust we're now all in agreement on that point.

Please treat with the utmost caution any fellow human who doesn't get miffed or bothered by the 67. These people are not worthy of your friendship, trust or time. Being cautious and cynical is a perfectly healthy disposition, so don't let pesky do-gooders and annoying optimists try to change your mind. It's an irrefutable fact-checked fact that our often challenging and troubling world would be a happier and cuddlier place if those on the list ceased to be a presence within it.

I would also urge you to begin making your own list. If you find yourself experiencing that impending sense of losing the will to live because of the cretins and clowns who lurk among us with their batty and irritating ways, write it down. I promise you, putting pen to paper is a revelation. I genuinely believe that most people have a 67 within them, so get scribbling. Perhaps, over time, our collective works will create an entire library dedicated solely to the crimes of human idiocy.

Future generations will thank us for supplying the definitive guidelines on how life can be immeasurably improved.

I'm regularly asked about those who didn't make the list. How did I pick and choose and whittle that number down to a simple 67? It wasn't easy and the process of deciding who was in and who didn't quite make the grade was long and tiring. I promise you, I wrestled with hundreds more who came close and I spent many dark nights playing devil's advocate with my own soul in order to be sure that I had created the mother list. As a parting shot, I thought I would share with you just *some* of the ones that got away.

- Myleene Klass. For no other reason than those weird faces she pulls whenever she plays the piano. Is she in pain? Or is this the look of creative joy? Either way, stop it.
- Anyone doing the backstroke in an already crowded swimming pool. You're not an octopus and space here is limited. Have some respect.
- Tailgaters. If I brake, you die. Ergo, you're a moron.
- People who carry a bottle of water like it's a fashion accessory (almost always men). Don't swing it, or juggle with it, just hold the damn thing. Better still, drink it.
- Fiona Bruce. No particular reason.
- Bar staff who don't notice that you're next to be served. Knowing who has been queuing for eight hours is actually part of the job.
- Sushi. It's nice. It's *really* nice. It's just not game-changingly nice.
- Shop staff who slap the change down on the counter despite the fact that you're holding out your hand ready to receive it.

- Booking a local taxi only for the company to send a minibus rather than a car. I'm not going on a coach trip. A car would have done just fine. Sitting in a twenty-seater, on my own, is not a good look.
- The fact that, looking back, John Major seems like quite a nice bloke.
- People who think it's cool to not like Apple products.
- Anyone who refers to radio presenters as DJs. If you play music, you're a DJ. If you don't, you're not. It's that simple. Like a plumber isn't a bricklayer, they just work in similar places.
- Brits using the word cookies instead of biscuits. What's that all about?
- People who drop lit cigarettes and don't stub them out. What are you, some sort of pyromaniac?
- Professional footballers who religiously cross their chest before a match. It's a football match, not a christening.
- Robert Peston. If someone started talking to you in a bar with that voice, you'd leave.
- The insane penchant of restaurants for serving food on a chopping board or a piece of stone. I'm not a caveman, a plate will do nicely.
- High-fives in cricket. Not the done thing, boys. Save that for baseball.
- People with a constant smile on their face as they walk down the road. Creepy.
- That single-sheet page you get in a broadsheet newspaper. Why?
- People who eat while you're on the phone to them. Mucky.
- Companies that won't let you take out a direct debit on YOUR day of choosing. Why?

- People who *walk* up escalators. A very clever person designed them to save you doing exactly that.
- Cretins who add loud rock music to YouTube videos for no apparent reason.
- The schools edition of *Question Time*. I have no interest in knowing what an eleven-year-old thinks about Article 50.
- Singers who call themselves R&B performers when they are actually just *pop* singers.
- Websites that require you to register before using them. Piss off.
- The daft obsession (mostly from government) with name reversing: when did the Scottish Police become Police Scotland? Or the England Team, Team England? Who decided to add this curious French vibe to our language?
- Restaurants that give you near-on frozen butter. This will only result in the total annihilation of your bread roll.
- People who talk in esoteric tones about an album being great when what they really mean is they like track 4. This is because they know bugger all about music and haven't actually listened to the rest of it.
- Supermarkets that give you too much stuff. I don't need three for one. Have they never heard of Western excess and waste? It's quite a debate right now.
- People who don't know how to dress when going to the theatre. Tracksuits are not acceptable clobber.
- Folk who say *lend* when they mean *borrow*. You wouldn't say hot when you mean cold, so pack it in.
- Helplines that close at 5 p.m. and don't function at weekends. That really isn't much help.
- Fellow passengers on the train who continue to talk loudly

while the guard is making an announcement. Please shut up. This could be important.

- Adults who opt for snowboarding over skiing. Do stop, you're not fourteen.
- Folk who act up and start pulling stupid faces when a TV camera picks them out at a sports event or telly show.
- Men who whistle. Why are you doing this? Why?
- People who stand at zebra crossings with no intention of crossing.
- Anyone who wears a hat indoors. When did that become OK?
- Middle-class people opting for the new trend of dropping theirs Ts (battery, community, British, are common targets). Please stop, you sound like an arse.
- The inventor of the loyalty card. You are a cunning con merchant. Having to spend the equivalent of about thirteen grand in order to get a free DVD is *not* a good deal and won't buy my loyalty.
- Celebrities on those talking heads programmes pretending to reminisce about stuff they clearly have no knowledge of other than the script they were handed three days before recording.
- Bloggers. They are not the oracle, they are just the opinions of an individual, so quit quoting them on the radio as if they are the Press Association.
- Anyone over the age of twelve who thinks it's acceptable to use a scooter. I recently clocked a guy of about fifty gliding through the streets of Salford as if it was the most normal thing in the world. It's not cool, it's disturbing.
- Mobile phone companies. If I'm calling with an ongoing

problem, how about coming up with a system that will allow me to speak to the *same* person each time? This means I don't have to repeat the same story to forty-seven different people in the event of you being unable to sort out my issue. Which is highly likely.

- Writers of medical dramas. A senior surgeon never went for coffee with the porter or discussed his love life with the cleaner. I know class cohesion is a romantic idea, but it doesn't happen.

- Training days. Did you ever meet anyone who learnt anything from one of these events? Companies pay thousands per day for this kind of hooey. Maybe time for a rethink.

- Anyone who pronounces foreign words in a thick foreign accent. You sound ridiculous.

- Mini roundabout pests. It's still a roundabout. You're meant to go *around* it, not over it. That's why it's called a roundabout.

- Shop assistants who hand you your change – notes, coins and receipt – all in one pile onto your palm. I don't do balancing.

- People who work in electrical stores who know nothing about products that are sold in electrical stores.

- Conspiracy theorists. Believing that the Queen is a shape-shifting lizard, Jay-Z is a time-travelling vampire, the Middle East war is a plot by the New World Order to deliberately destabilise the planet so that the Illuminati can rule our lives and the internet is policed by a shady cartel of mind-reading stoats is not only illogical, it's completely insane.

ACKNOWLEDGEMENTS

When I first came up with the idea of putting this book together, I was with my friend Danny Wallace. Neither of us can quite remember who coined the title name, although I suspect it was Dan (he suspects it was me). Regardless, in the time it's taken me to complete this book, Dan has written about ten of his own. If ever there was an inspiring example of graft and getting on with it, this is your man. Thank you, Dan.

My mates Laura Marshall, Mike Hanson and Will Guyatt. All three very generously allowed me to retell various stories and anecdotes, sometimes to their own detriment. Laura is still addicted to *Geordie Shore* and Mike continues to dress up in other people's clothes. Guyatt also went above and beyond in helping me frame stories, checked my spelling and taught me that semi-colons are not compulsory in every sentence.

Special thanks to Alan Hyde for allowing me to impart some of his own moments of social dissatisfaction. He remains the most trusted man on Planet Earth.

My business partner Kevin Job for allowing me to virtually disappear while I put this book together. He worked many eighteen-hour days purely so that I could sweat over my keyboard and change the world.

My former LBC producer Alex Hazlehurst, whose contribution to this book is precisely zero. That said, she was patient enough to listen while I whittled on about the pretentious struggles of being a writer. Similarly, my current producer Tom Watters (who I'm not sure ever believed I was writing a book) was also happy to grin at me as I regaled him with stories about the process.

I would like to thank Iain Dale and all at Biteback Publishing. Particular thanks to Olivia Beattie for the editing and occasional counselling. And to James Stephens for being the perfect gentleman in understanding my nervous request for a deadline extension.

I'd also like to thank the 67. Without your infuriating ways, my life may well be a smoother affair, but, arguably, much less interesting. Your existence continues to provide me with endless amounts of material.

Finally, to my wife Emma, who must have now forgotten what a weekend looks like. I'm all yours again. Until the next one.

ABOUT THE AUTHOR

Ian Collins is best known as the host of *The Late Show* on LBC. He is a journalist, comedy writer and a regular pundit on television and radio.

He also has the curious distinction of being played by Bradley Cooper in a Hollywood movie.

67 People I'd Like to Slap is his first book.

Ian lives in Kent with his wife and family.

Follow Ian on Twitter: @IanCollinsUK